HENRY FIELDING
THE TENTATIVE REALIST

*Oxford University Press, Ely House, London W.*1

GLASGOW NEW YORK TORONTO MELBOURNE WELLINGTON
CAPE TOWN SALISBURY IBADAN NAIROBI LUSAKA ADDIS ABABA
BOMBAY CALCUTTA MADRAS KARACHI LAHORE DACCA
KUALA LUMPUR HONG KONG TOKYO

HENRY FIELDING

THE TENTATIVE REALIST

By

MICHAEL IRWIN

CLARENDON PRESS

OXFORD

1967

Made and printed in Great Britain by
William Clowes and Sons, Limited, London and Beccles

To My Mother

PREFACE

ONE of the things I am trying to show in this book is that Fielding was a didactic writer, a moralist, from the very beginning of his literary career. The best evidence for this is the regularity with which he returns in his work to a number of specific social and ethical issues. It is the consistency and frequency, rather than the quality, of his comments on these topics that most clearly reveal his moral preoccupation. Logically, therefore, I should have begun this book with a massive, thickly-illustrated chapter demonstrating chronologically the persistence of the relevant themes. Since this promised to be very dull I chose instead to risk a methodological loop. My comparatively brief account of the ideas in question I have illustrated as far as possible from the journalism of Fielding's middle period (c. 1738–41). In the chapters discussing the plays, which nearly all came earlier, and the novels, which of course were later, I have tried to develop the various points I am concerned with by means of quotations which closely parallel those previously given from the journalistic writings. In other words I have shown the continuity of Fielding's moral interest implicitly rather than explicitly.

No attempt is made here to evaluate the plays, the journalism or the minor narrative works. They are considered almost entirely for their illustration of tendencies in Fielding's writing which were to be important to his development as a novelist. My concern is with the three major novels. I want to discuss how they came to be the kind of works they are, and how they function for the modern reader.

The main substance of this book was originally an Oxford B.Litt. thesis. The additions—most notably the final chapter—grow largely from my reading of E. H. Gombrich's

Art and Illusion. I hope I have not misrepresented any of Professor Gombrich's ideas in translating them from art to literature.

I would like to thank Jonathan Wordsworth of Exeter College, Oxford, for helpful suggestions about the structure of the book. I would also like to thank my wife, without whose help it would not have been completed for at least another year.

MICHAEL IRWIN

Smith College, July 1966

NOTE ON WORKS CITED

The following abbreviations have been used:

ELH	*Journal of English Literary History*
MLN	*Modern Language Notes*
MLQ	*Modern Language Quarterly*
N and Q	*Notes and Queries*
PQ	*Philological Quarterly*
PMLA	*Publications of the Modern Language Association of America*
RES	*The Review of English Studies*

As many of the quotations from Fielding's work are very brief I have made the footnotes as precise as possible by referring to the volume and page number of the Henley edition, which includes virtually all Fielding's important work. But since there is a full and scholarly edition of *The Covent-Garden Journal* (ed. Gerard Edward Jensen, New Haven and London, 1915, 2 vols.), containing material not to be found in Henley, I have also made use of that. For the benefit of readers who cannot get hold of the Henley edition I have added, after each quotation from the novels, the book and chapter number found in all editions.

Where Cross is cited in the footnotes the reference is to *The History of Henry Fielding*, by W. L. Cross, New Haven, 1918, 3 vols. When referring to *The Spectator*, I give the number of the issue according to the Everyman edition (ed. G. Gregory Smith, London and New York, 1907, 4 vols.).

CONTENTS

I

INTRODUCTION

THIS book will try to show how Fielding's novels became what they are. It rests on two assumptions: first, that it is possible to find out a great deal about what Fielding was trying to do in the novels, and how he was trying to do it; second, that, since he was building up a new literary form by trial and error, an examination of his technical successes and failures will reveal something about the potentialities of the novel in general.

The first of these assumptions probably requires more explanation than the second. Fielding's intentions as a novelist, then, are unusually clear, partly because he so often states them explicitly, partly because his entire career as a writer shows such a marked uniformity of general purpose.

The curious notion that Fielding was a genial libertine, a notion which persisted well into the present century, until finally disposed of by Cross, naturally tended to obscure the obvious fact that he is above all an ethical writer. By now, of course, this ethical concern has been generally recognized, and critics have even begun to point out that the novels have a specifically moral intention. Professor Sherburn claims that *Amelia*, at least, is so much a didactic work that 'enunciation of ethical principles pre-occupies the author rather more than plot, character, or dramatic effect';[1] M. C. Battestin has shown that the meaning and structure of *Joseph Andrews* are similarly dependent on a moral purpose.[2]

As yet, however, there have been no attempts at a comprehensive account of this aspect of Fielding's work, merely observations about particular novels. Only if his

[1] George Sherburn, 'Fielding's Social Outlook', *Eighteenth-Century English Literature*, ed. J. L. Clifford, New York and London, 1959, p. 265.
[2] In *The Moral Basis of Fielding's Art*, Middletown, Connecticut, 1959.

dramatic and journalistic writings are taken into consideration does it become possible to understand the full nature and
scope of his didactic purpose. Perhaps it would be as well at
the outset to deny the view, sometimes advanced, that these
works are 'unjustly neglected'. As far as their intrinsic
merits are concerned the neglect is very reasonable. Taken
together, though, they do have value for what they reveal of
Fielding's thought in the years prior to his first novel. They
establish, beyond question, the intensity and continuity of
his moral preoccupation. Certain didactic themes recur
again and again, introduced regularly into the plays,
expounded directly in editorial articles and occasional essays.
And these are the same themes which are eventually to become the basis of the novels. This book will isolate and
classify these themes, with a view to showing just how important they are to Fielding's work.

It will be shown that even his lighter dramas contain an
important moral element. In some of the plays he introduces
extraneous episodes solely to make a didactic point. Even in
an amoral artificial comedy he will invoke realistic ethical
standards. Regularly, in fact, Fielding's moral intention
takes precedence over the demands of form.

It is hardly surprising, then, that in the novels, where he is
free to develop his own form, the didactic purpose is an
important shaping factor. As Sherburn and Battestin suggest, and as the following chapters will show in greater
detail, each of the narratives is tailored to meet the demands
of a moral plan.

Failure to realize this fact is one of several reasons behind
the frequent misunderstanding of Fielding's work. It has
been rightly acknowledged that the new medium he evolved
was a synthesis of techniques borrowed from existing
genres: the picaresque tale, the occasional essay, the artificial
comedy. But it has been wrongly assumed that the nature of
this synthesis was determined chiefly by aesthetic considerations. Fielding did have theoretical ideas about the requirements of prose narrative, of course, but his primary concern
was always didactic. His choice of techniques within the
novels was usually dictated by the cast of his moral views.
Some of them could be represented only in terms of action,

others only in terms of character. Some of them demanded a formal embodiment, some a realistic. The form Fielding developed involved an uneasy compromise between these various pressures, and can be adequately studied only with reference to them.

The chief difficulty in the way of such a study is the unaccommodating nature of Fielding's didacticism. Although his views derive from the worthiest Christian ideals, they are distinctly commonplace in themselves. Moreover they emerge less often in basic statements of principle than in a miscellany of relatively trivial observations on a variety of specific topics. They are of interest, then, almost solely for their importance to Fielding's imaginative work; and this importance is most conveniently demonstrated in terms of the frequency with which such minor points recur.

The difficulty for the critic, however, is only methodological. The ideas concerned *can* be established. So too, if less precisely, can the literary influences which helped to determine the character of his novels. It is possible to indicate, at least roughly, the sources of his narrative methods.

Here a caveat is necessary. There has already been a good deal of research into Fielding's narrative theory. But the emphasis on theory has been at the expense of an understanding of his practice. In *Amelia*, after all, he tacitly abandons many of the major principles set out in *Joseph Andrews* and *Tom Jones*. There are several possible explanations for this change of policy, but the most obvious is that the chapters on the 'comi-prosai-epic' in the earlier books were basically little more than *ad hoc* self-justification. Fielding could not have helped realizing that his work bore dangerous superficial similarities to the 'Romances' he condemned.

It is not very helpful to follow Fielding's own lead by talking, in Aristotelian terms, of fable, action, and characters. These are entities which the crudest narrative writer would have difficulty in omitting. A better starting-point is a consideration of the specific techniques Fielding uses, say, to link two chapters, to recount an episode, to demonstrate some good quality in his hero. He was not, of course, inventing but assembling a new narrative language. Essentially the novel was concocted from ingredients familiar in existing literary forms. It is possible to deduce something about Fielding's particular choice of ingredients because his previous work as a writer provides helpful clues, and because a good deal is known, in one way and another, about his reading and his literary preferences.

Each of Fielding's novels, then, is a collage. A knowledge of his literary background will show where he culled the different bits and pieces he makes use of. A knowledge of his didactic motives will reveal the organizing principle behind the assembling of these various fragments. It should then be possible to decide how far the finished work of art is a coherent, self-consistent whole, and how far it fulfils Fielding's stated intentions. Where there is a disparity between what he attempts and what he achieves it may well be because he has misjudged the requirements of his emerging form.

It is not easy, however, to make a dispassionate assessment of Fielding's successes and failures as an innovator. The rather obvious programme outlined in this chapter would surely have been carried out long ago, were it not for three main difficulties. One of these has already been mentioned. There was clearly no possibility of making a serious study of Fielding as long as it was assumed that he was a bawdy writer.

In the second place his novels tend to elicit a rather horrible stock response from British readers. The presence, especially in *Tom Jones*, of squires and huntsmen, coaches and inns, induces a nostalgic euphoria that blurs critical insight and usually seeks expression in metaphors about Old Wine and God's Fresh Air. This attitude precludes response to the more interesting aspects of Fielding's achievement, and explains the fact that so much of the critical work about the novels has been trivial and misconceived. Once a critic has decided that they are 'rollicking' he is unlikely to get much farther with them. Who would look for tentative experiment in a 'rollicking' work?

Objective analysis of Fielding, then, requires that this stock response be subdued. But it also demands a second, and much more difficult, feat of suppression : the suppression of some of the essential instincts of the novel reader. The stock response, of course, is induced by various elements in the narratives which happen to have acquired irrelevant emotional associations. But the account of the books given by various critics shows that this is closely linked with another reaction—the unconscious tendency to read the novels not as the uncertain, though purposeful, experimental works which they are, but as modern works *manqués*. It is easy—irrationally—to feel that Fielding was trying to write a twentieth-century novel and falling short of it in certain respects. But naturally he was doing no such thing. He was proffering different sorts of information in different ways, and for a number of distinct purposes. His hope was that each resultant 'history' would take on life in the minds of his readers—that the different kinds of information would fuse into a coherent picture of reality. Since he was a pioneer in this difficult art it would have been surprising if he had been uniformly successful. As he tries to work out his conception some parts of it—unpredictably from his own point of view—'come alive', while others fail to do so. Yet to see why, or even exactly where, this happens, is surprisingly difficult. The power of projection—the power of filling in gaps and rounding out hints—which is probably a condition of understanding any sort of art, invests the novels with a kind of life which is to some extent anachronistic and alien to their real meaning. The reader refuses, so to speak, to register all the inconsistencies of tone or narrative level which confront him. He instinctively takes up a stance which reduces the contradictions to a minimum. He forgets passages which seem irrelevant or discordant; he assigns to the characters what motive or complexity they may seem, by contemporary standards, to lack. His estimate of the nature and purpose of the novels, therefore, may be quite at variance with the author's intentions.

The references here to 'real meaning' and 'the author's intentions' are critical shorthand, not attempts to beg any questions. Clearly a reader can be 'right' about the novels and Fielding 'wrong'. And in any case this disparity between intention and achievement afflicts many, perhaps all, works of art. The point in this case is that since Fielding was trying to build up a new medium from scratch, the reader's automatic tendency to help him out imaginatively, to assist in the illusion, may lead him to respond irrelevantly to aspects of the narrative of which the author is not fully in control. It is possible to read a largely subjective life into his books.

A roughly comparable error has been attributed to certain of the adverse critics of *Paradise Lost*. It is said that they react to God and Satan too much as if they were characters in a novel, to be judged by twentieth-century standards of right and wrong. Whether this particular charge is true is another matter, but certainly this is a possible, and perhaps even to some extent an unavoidable, kind of error. Generally speaking, the modern reader will learn to understand a work from the point of view of the age in which it was written, only after he has already enjoyed it from his own point of view. In Fielding's case, of course, the gap between the instinctive and the 'objective' reaction is relatively narrow, but it is still a source of misunderstanding. The recent film of *Tom Jones*, for example, though entertaining enough, represented this easy-going view, which has by now become stereotyped.

Because they make a conscious effort to avoid the kind of error described above, the ensuing analyses may seem unsympathetic. It should be made clear at once, therefore, that this book does not aim at a total estimate of Fielding's achievement. In any case the plays and minor writings are referred to chiefly for the light they shed on the novels. But even the novels are not radically reassessed. Many of their positive qualities—their humour, their satire, their humanity—are taken for granted. If the emphasis here very often seems to fall on Fielding's limitations it is not in an attempt to belittle his greatness as a writer and as a man. E. H. Gombrich says: 'In the study of art no less than in the study of man, the mysteries of success are frequently best revealed through an investigation of failures.'[1] Fielding's books have a deceptive air of simplicity. The following chapters, by drawing attention to the frequency with which he miscalculated, or fell into contradictions, will try to suggest how much invention and good judgement was needed

---

[1] *Art and Illusion*, London, 1960, p. 67. I hope it is apparent that some of the arguments and formulations in this chapter owe a great deal to Professor Gombrich's book.

to make his novels the works of art they are. But the account of the books given here cannot, and is not intended to, stand on its own. It is designed not to supersede the traditional account of the novels, but to be superimposed on it, amending it only in a few important respects.

II

FIELDING'S MORAL POSITION

MUCH of the thought of eighteenth-century England involved a fundamental ambiguity. Reason was confidently proposed as the sole arbiter of conduct, but there remained an instinctive confidence in traditions and beliefs originally derived from Authority. The result was a series of compromises.

Since English society at the time was predominantly Christian, philosophical, moral, and even political theory were largely subsumed under religious thought. And in that crucial sphere the tendency towards compromise was particularly marked. Deism, one logical conclusion of a purely rational approach to theology, created controversy but made few converts, and was nearly forgotten by the middle of the century. Militant atheism remained almost unheard of. The general attitude of the Church was epitomized by the willingness of Locke, the thinker most influential in the period, to accept the authority both of pure intellect and of the Bible. This partial reliance on dogma meant that the change in contemporary Anglicanism was limited to one of emphasis.

None the less the change was an important one. The new belief in the capacity of the unassisted intellect to find the way to salvation had several notable corollaries. The Deity had to be deducible merely from the observation of external phenomena; hence the concept of Natural Religion. Since intellectual abilities vary, the beliefs necessary for salvation were reduced to a few fundamentals: Locke suggested that an acknowledgement that Christ was the Messiah was the only essential article of Faith, all the rest stemming from it. But since the heathen is denied any tidings about Revelation, salvation for him had in justice to be obtainable through good deeds alone.

The general trend, then, was to reduce Christianity to a few basic imperatives. Revelation and the supernatural element were much less stressed. Works were considered far more important than faith.

These attitudes, which reflected the wide current reliance on the individual intelligence, were most systematically advanced by the latitudinarian divines. All such preachers were essentially rationalistic in their approach, South, for example, contending that 'all Arguments whatsoever against Experience are fallacious.'[1] Tillotson states: 'Nothing ought to be received as a revelation from God which plainly contradicts the principles of natural religion.'[2] It is repeatedly emphasized that virtue is natural to man, and the practice of it the only way to salvation. Tillotson goes so far as to say: 'A right faith is wholly in order to a good life, and is of no value any farther than it hath an influence upon it.'[3] The latitudinarians accept the logic of this position by stating categorically that the virtuous heathen will be saved.

Virtue itself they equate with Charity, which arises from an instinctive sympathy with the joys and sorrows of one's fellow man and a desire to assist him. Barrow asserts that there have always been many charitable persons ' ... heartily desiring the publick good, and compassionating the evils of mankind, ready with their best endeavours to procure and promote the one, to prevent and remove the other ... '[4] Such a benevolent disposition is called 'Good-nature' by several of the latitudinarians, and the term came into general use. *The Spectator*, for instance, devotes two articles to a consideration of 'Good-nature'.[5]

Since charitable actions spring from a natural sympathy, it follows that performing them will give pleasure. The idea, common to the latitudinarians, is aptly summed up by Isaac Barrow:

[1] Robert South, *Thirty Six Sermons and Discourses*, 5th ed., Dublin, 1720, i.2.
[2] Quoted by Leslie Stephen, *English Thought in the Eighteenth Century*, London, 1876, i.78.
[3] Quoted by Battestin, *The Moral Basis of Fielding's Art*, p. 20.
[4] *The Works of Isaac Barrow*, London, 1741, ii.83.
[5] In nos. 169 and 177.

... Nature ... hath ... made the Communication of Benefits to others, to be accompanied with a very delicious Relish upon the Mind of him that practises it; nothing indeed carrying with it a more pure and savory Delight than Beneficence. A man may be VIRTUOUSLY VOLUPTUOUS, AND A LAUDABLE EPICURE BY DOING MUCH GOOD.[1]

An emphasis on charity and an avoidance of dogma, then, were the chief characteristics of the latitudinarians. But it must be admitted that the group cannot be very rigidly defined. Although they provided much of the Christian argument in the Deist controversy they had in fact a great deal in common with their opponents. Both sides believed in the existence of a Deity, in Natural Virtue, and in the priority of Reason. Argument centred chiefly on the extent to which divine inscrutability should be invoked. Latitudinarianism is really nothing more than the Church of England formulation of the contemporary tolerance and rationalism.

But again, since England was very much an Anglican country, it was probably the latitudinarian influence which did most to condition the public attitude to Christianity and morality in the first half of the eighteenth century. At least until the advent of Whitefield and Wesley the dogmatic and mystical sides of religion were very much subordinated to the moral side. The sermons of the Low Church divines show one effect of the new system of priorities. As compared with the homilies of the previous century they are much less formal in tone, much less grandiloquent and doctrinaire. They are written to appeal directly to the intelligence of the ordinary educated man. It was no doubt this lowering of tone which helped to encourage the notable increase in secular moral writing at the beginning of the eighteenth century; the language of didacticism had moved much closer to that of everyday cultivated speech. Soon *The Tatler* and *The Spectator* were making literary and commercial capital out of stylish moralizing and elegant admonishment. By the time Fielding came to write, an ethical intention was essential to any serious writer and open exhortation was a commonplace.

---

[1] Quoted in *The Covent-Garden Journal*, i.308.

I

M. C. Battestin, in his recent study of *Joseph Andrews*, claims that 'Fielding's ethic has been traced to its source in the popular latitudinarianism of his day.'[1] If he is implying that Fielding's beliefs were specifically derived from the Low Church homilists he is over-simplifying the issue. Many of their attitudes—as was indicated above—were generally current, and shared even by the Deists. It is impossible, therefore, despite a number of verbal parallels, to tell when Fielding is drawing particularly upon the latitudinarians' work, and when merely expressing a widely-accepted view which they happen to share.

None the less he was clearly an admirer of the Low Church homilists. His library contained the works of Chillingworth, South, Barrow, Clarke, and Tillotson. In *The Champion* he claims that the two last have amply demonstrated 'the immortality of the soul, and the certainty of a future state'.[2] In the poem *Of True Greatness* he extols Hoadly;[3] and regularly in his journalism he quotes South, whom he praises as wittier than Congreve,[4] and above all 'our favourite Dr. Barrow'. Like the latitudinarians he is opposed to the misanthropic pessimism of Hobbes and Mandeville,[5] and to the Deists' denial of Revelation and of the life to come.[6] He uses the argument previously employed by Tillotson, South, and Barrow, among others, by which earthly suffering is made evidence of a future existence.[7]

But from the point of view of his imaginative writing by far the most significant attitude he shares with the latitudinarians is a belief in the paramount importance of Charity. In *An Inquiry into the Causes of the Late Increase in Robbers* he asserts: 'Indeed the passion of love or benevolence . . . seems to be the only human passion that is in itself simply and absolutely good . . . '[8] Regularly in his works he uses the term 'Good-nature' in a sense similar to that in which it is employed by the homilists. It is worth quoting Fielding's

[1] *The Moral Basis of Fielding's Art*, p. 11.
[2] Henley ed., xv.163.   [3] Henley ed., xii.256.
[4] *The Covent-Garden Journal*, i.243.   [5] (e.g.) Henley ed., xv.94, 165 ff.
[6] (e.g.) Henley ed., xv.161 ff.   [7] (e.g.) Henley ed., xv.218.
[8] Henley ed., xiii.110.

own definitions of the word. That in *The Champion* has close affinities with Barrow's comment on charity quoted above: 'Good-nature is a delight in the happiness of mankind, and a concern at their misery, with a desire, as much as possible, to procure the former, and avert the latter; and this, with a constant regard to desert.'[1] There is a similar statement in *An Essay on the Knowledge of the Characters of Men*:

Good-nature is that benevolent and amiable temper of mind, which disposes us to feel the misfortunes, and enjoy the happiness of others; and, consequently, pushes us on to promote the latter, and prevent the former; and that without any abstract contemplation on the beauty of virtue, and without the allurements or terrors of religion.[2]

The qualifications to these definitions are not important. In the first example Fielding is concerned to establish the necessity for discrimination since he is to go on to suggest that bringing a criminal to justice 'is, perhaps, the best natured office we can perform to society'. In the second he wishes to make it clear that the feeling in question is natural and spontaneous. A third definition, in the poem *Of Good-nature*, is limited to the essential qualities:

What by this name, then, shall be understood?
What? but the glorious lust of doing good?
The heart that finds its happiness to please
Can feel another's pain, and taste his ease;
The cheek that with another's joy can glow,
Turn pale and sicken with another's woe . . . [3]

These definitions are not, however, of great practical significance. In *The Champion* Fielding says: 'I do not know a better general definition of virtue, than that it is a delight in doing good . . . '[4] Good-nature for him, then, as for the latitudinarians, is practically synonymous with virtue itself, and merely provides a convenient label for the warm and active sympathy which he regards as the foundation of all morality.

[1] Henley ed., xv.258.   [2] Henley ed., xiv.285.
[3] Henley ed., xii.258–9.   [4] Henley ed., xv.136.

The use of the word 'delight' in two of these descriptions suggests that incentive to the benevolent disposition which Fordyce was to call 'Self-approving Joy'.[1] Fielding quotes Barrow's passage on Christian epicureanism in *The Covent-Garden Journal* and frequently advances the same idea in his own terms: '. . . what can give greater Happiness to a good Mind, than the Reflexion on having relieved the Misery or contributed to the well being, of his Fellow-Creature.'[2] Vice, on the other hand, being antipathetic to man's natural moral sense, must ultimately cause uneasiness, as Fielding suggests in the Preface to the *Miscellanies*: 'The same righteous judge [= conscience] always annexes a bitter anxiety to the purchases of guilt, whilst it adds a double sweetness to the enjoyments of innocence and virtue . . .'[3] Regularly the corollary is stressed:

. . . if we strip virtue and vice of all their outward ornaments and appearances, and view them both naked . . . we shall, I trust, find virtue to have in her every thing that is truly valuable, to be a constant mistress, a faithful friend, and a pleasant companion; while vice will appear a tawdry, painted harlot, within, all foul and impure, enticing only at a distance, the possession of her certainly attended with uneasiness, pain, disease, poverty, and dishonour.[4]

These few basic ideas on charity, constantly expressed and re-expressed in Fielding's work, constitute what might be called the positive side of his didactic beliefs. But although frequently at pains to propagate these constructive moral views, he is more often, and more characteristically, a satirist. His simple precept of active charitableness becomes significant in his writings partly because of the host of negative attitudes it implies.

Since Fielding's cardinal virtues are kindness and concern for others, his cardinal sins are naturally cruelty and egotism. He concludes an attack on 'roasting' in *The Champion*:

If we consider this diversion in the worst light, it will appear to be no other than a delight in seeing the miseries, misfortunes, and frailties

[1] Quoted by R. S. Crane, 'Genealogy of the Man of Feeling', *ELH*, i. (1934), 205.
[2] *The Covent-Garden Journal*, ii.9.   [3] Henley ed., xii.244.
[4] *The Champion*, Henley ed., xv.167.

of mankind displayed; and a pleasure and joy conceived in their sufferings therein. A pleasure, perhaps, as inhuman, and which must arise from a nature as thoroughly corrupt and diabolical, as can possibly pollute the mind of man.[1]

Fielding often stresses his high regard for women; his sexual ethic, therefore, is less concerned with abstract notions of chastity than with an insistence that the woman must not be made a victim of treachery:

This Letter is designed for the Use of the loveliest, and, I sincerely think, the best Part of the Creation, who seldom stray but when they are misled by Men; by whom they are deceived, corrupted, betrayed, and often *brought to Destruction, both of Body and Soul*. In the Sequel therefore, I will treat in general of these Corrupters of the Innocence of Women; and of the extreme Baseness as well as Cruelty of this Practice, how favourably soever the World may please to receive it.[2]

Similarly it is because of the slaughter and misery that they cause that 'Great Men' are often the object of Fielding's satire. Even ill-treatment of animals is attacked in a special article in *The Champion*.[3] Fielding could tolerate no form of cruelty.

For him the types of egotism are the avaricious and the ambitious man. He condemns miserliness more often and more virulently than any other single vice. In *The Champion*, to quote an obvious instance, two whole editorials are given up to a dream-vision satirizing avarice.[4] A certain amount of ambition Fielding is prepared to tolerate; he says of Virtue that: 'Ambition itself, if moderate, she will countenance, she will not indeed permit you, by all means whatever, to rise and advance yourself; yet she has been known to raise some to the highest dignities in the State, in the Army, and in the Law.'[5] When he attacks ambition, which is frequently, it is on the assumption that it is shameless and unscrupulous, as in the case of the ruthless general, the fawning courtier, or the crafty politician.

Yet that the miser and the self-seeker frequently thrive, and enjoy a good reputation in the world, is a fact Fielding

---

[1] Henley ed., xv.243.   [2] *The Covent-Garden Journal*, i.255.
[3] Henley ed., xv.252 ff.   [4] Henley ed., xv.121 ff.
[5] *The Champion*, Henley ed., xv.167.

cannot gainsay. He attributes their success to a capacity for acting one part and playing another. Hypocrisy, therefore, becomes an important and recurrent target. In *The Champion* he publishes what purports to be a letter from a hypocrite:

> My temper is so far from being inclined to good nature, that I always triumph in other people's misfortunes, yet, at the expense of a little verbal pity ... I pass for a very good-natured person ... you already, I believe, conclude that I have a heart not too charitably disposed; and yet I am the only person of my acquaintance who will tell you that I am not the most charitable creature alive; for though I never give any thing myself, yet I always abuse others for not giving more.[1]

Fielding was not alone in thinking that the virtuous man was particularly vulnerable to this kind of dissimulation on the part of the vicious.[2] He complains in *The Champion*:

> Honest and undesigning men of very good understanding would be always liable to the attacks of cunning and artful knaves, into whose snares we are as often seduced by the openness and goodness of the heart, as by the weakness of the head. True wisdom is commonly attended with a simplicity of manners, which betrays a worthy man to a tricking shuffler, of a much inferior capacity.[3]

It was to protect the ingenuous that he wrote *An Essay on the Knowledge of the Characters of Men*, which was designed to show how to detect a man's true disposition by careful observation. More generally, in nearly all his works he strives to unmask affectation and deceit. Much of his best writing defends real, as against professed, ethical standards.

If these various aspects of conduct with which Fielding occupies himself have a common denominator it is that they all involve behaviour between people; his chief didactic concern was social morality. This fact has an important implication for his imaginative writing. As the various vices and virtues he is to depict are essentially those of everyday life, they can only be fully realized in drama or fiction if the context is reasonably close to common experience. Thus the

---

[1] Henley ed., xv.95.   [2] Cf. *The Spectator*, no. 245.
[3] Henley ed., xv.217.

fulfilment of Fielding's didactic purpose demands a large degree of realism.

2

Because Fielding was a very practical moralist he naturally tended to attack particular evils visible in society. Explicit and detailed social criticism was already a literary commonplace. Although much of the didactic content of *The Tatler* and *The Spectator* is confined to gentle satire against the affectations of fashionable life, there is an underlying awareness of 'that desperate State of Vice and Folly into which the Age is fallen'.[1] The Spectator often censures the manners and morals of the day with real severity; and he makes a host of particular criticisms. He condemns duelling, 'wenching', and the degeneracy of the stage. He attacks the empty life of the town, and the fatuity of masquerades and Italian opera.[2]

The nature and the effectiveness of these criticisms are aptly summarized in Gay's well-known comment on Steele:

> There is this noble difference between him and all the rest of our polite and gallant authors: the latter have endeavoured to please the age by falling in with them, and encouraging them in their fashionable vices and false notions of things . . . Bickerstaff ventured to tell the town that they were a parcel of fops, fools and vain coquettes; but in such a manner as even pleased them, and made them more than half inclined to believe that he spoke truth.[3]

Gay himself indulges in similar social criticism, and he often shows genuine bitterness in his moral satire:

> That wretch, to gain an equipage and place,
> Betray'd his sister to a lewd embrace.
> This coach, that with the blazon'd 'scutcheon glows,
> Vain of his unknown race, the coxcomb shows.
> Here the brib'd lawyer, sunk in velvet, sleeps;
> The starving orphan, as he passes, weeps . . . [4]

---

[1] *The Spectator*, no. 10; Everyman ed., i.38.

[2] (e.g.) *The Spectator*, nos. 8, 97, 182, 446.

[3] Quoted in the Introduction to *The Tatler*, ed. G. A. Aitken, London, 1898, i.xvii.

[4] 'Trivia' ii.575 ff., *The Poetical Works of John Gay*, ed. G. C. Faber, London, 1926, p. 78.

These lines illustrate Gay's constant awareness of the separation of merit and material reward. Everywhere in fashionable life vices were flourishing which would be punished among the poor. He sums up the injustice in *Polly*:

> All crimes are judg'd like fornication;
> While rich we are honest no doubt.
> Fine ladies can keep reputation,
> Poor lasses alone are found out.
> If justice had piercing eyes,
> Like ourselves to look within,
> She'd find power and wealth a disguise
> That shelter the worst of our kin.[1]

The Beggar's Opera is substantially an ironic expansion of the same idea.

It is unlikely that Fielding was influenced by any of these writers in regard to the matter of his moralizing. Their work is cited here partly to show that he had ample precedent in the sphere of social criticism, and partly to illustrate a widespread conviction in the period that contemporary life was riddled with triviality, corruption and injustice. The culminating expression of this disgust, Brown's *Estimate*, was not published until 1757. Virtually throughout Fielding's life, therefore, Vice and Folly were considered to be rife, and perhaps increasingly so. As a practical moralist he could hardly fail to perceive the many specific symptoms of degeneracy and condemn what he thought to be its causes.

It is important to an understanding of Fielding's social views to realize that he believed the immorality of the age to be very closely linked with its folly. In *A Charge to the Grand Jury*, for instance, he states the connexion:

Gentlemen, our newspapers, from the top of the page to the bottom, the corners of our streets up to the very eaves of our houses, present us with nothing but a view of masquerades, balls, and assemblies of various kinds, fairs, wells, gardens, &c., tending to promote idleness, extravagance, and immorality, among all sorts of people.

This fury after licentious and luxurious pleasures is grown to so enormous a height, that it may be called the characteristic of the present age. And it is an evil, gentlemen, of which it is neither easy nor pleasant to foresee all the consequences.[2]

[1] Ibid., p. 585.   [2] Henley ed., xiii.214–15.

Fielding's constant satire against particular and often trivial social targets represents, then, more than an idiosyncratic personal animus. Much of even his lightest satire stems from this fundamental conviction that the follies of society are tending to corrupt the nation's morals. Hence the repeated attacks on beaux, for example:

> The rotten beau, while smell'd along the room,
> Divides your nose 'twixt stenches and perfume . . . [1]

or on 'the wild coquette, and the censorious prude'.[2] The pastimes of society are also condemned; the drums and masquerades, the card-parties and ridottos, the Italian opera and the puerile theatrical entertainments.

It must be remembered that since 'the Age' to Fielding and his contemporaries meant only current High Society, this piecemeal criticism of manners and amusements amounts to a fairly comprehensive denunciation. *The Spectator* gives the diary of a rich spinster's typical week; there is a device for trifling away every hour of the day.[3] The way of life of many of the wealthy consisted solely of the diversions which Fielding ridicules.

But the corruptness of the age is very often attacked directly. In *The True Patriot* there is an indignant letter from Parson Adams:

> Can we expect to find charity in an age, when scarce any refuse to own the most profligate rapaciousness! when no man is ashamed of avowing the pursuit of riches through every dirty road and track? To speak out, in an age when every thing is venal; and when there is scarce one among the mighty who would not be equally ashamed at being thought not to set *some* price on himself, as he would at being imagined to set too low a one?[4]

Elections, preferment, even titles can be gained by money. Medicine and the law are corrupted, many of their practitioners being mere charlatans with a smattering of jargon. Dishonest lawyers and physicians feature again and again in

---

[1] *To John Hayes Esq.*, Henley ed., xii.275.

[2] *To a Friend*, Henley ed., xii.272.

[3] *The Spectator*, no. 323. Fielding uses the same idea in Wilson's story in *Joseph Andrews*.

[4] Henley ed., xiv.28.

Fielding's work. On occasion he implies that even the Church is tainted with this materialism.[1]

The result of this venality is that virtue and merit are at a discount:

> A very virtuous man may starve in Westminster Hall, or among the fair traders in the city, while the gentleman who would take fees in any cause, or sometimes on both sides of the same cause; and the trader who swears solemnly that he gets nothing by his silk at a crown a yard, and sells it afterwards for four shillings, will be pretty sure of growing rich.[2]

In the sphere of literature 'true wit and genius' are 'in a manner deposed, and imposters advanced in their place'[3]: '. . . for I think I may affirm with truth, that there is no one patron of true genius, nor the least encouragement left for it in this kingdom.'[4] There is a similar lack of encouragement for military merit. Fielding refers to: '. . . an acquaintance of mine, who, after he had served many campaigns in Flanders, and been wounded in Spain, with a generous heart and an empty pocket died in the King's Bench . . . '[5] Even marriage has become a way of making money. A pretty girl is a marketable property, disposed of to the highest bidder, and must resign herself to a loveless marriage.[6] Understandably such unions frequently lapse first into hatred and then into adultery. Altogether Fielding's writings imply a society that is decadent, frivolous, and often brutal.

It is by comparison with this gloomy picture of the town that his constant ideal of a peaceful country existence gains in persuasiveness. In one of Fielding's contributions to his sister's *Familiar Letters*, a Miss Lucy Rural, having received her friend's account of the delights of the city, replies that she is: '. . . convinced of the impertinence and stupidity of a town-life; and that we are not only more innocent, but much more merry and happy in the country.'[7] No doubt, as Battestin suggests, this theme partly derives from poetic

---

[1] (e.g.) *The Champion*, Henley ed., xv.273.
[2] *The Champion*, Henley ed., xv.172.
[3] *Familiar Letters*, Henley ed., xvi.28.
[4] *Familiar Letters*, Henley ed., xv.31.
[5] *The Champion*, Henley ed., xv.78.
[6] (e.g.) *The Champion*, Henley ed., xv.192.   [7] Henley ed., xvi.43.

tradition; but with Fielding the attitude is not purely a philosophical one. The country was preferable to the town not necessarily in absolute terms, but because the contemporary values of the town happened to be particularly vicious and inane. In any case the superior happiness of rural life is a constant theme in Fielding.

This rough categorizing of the social comments and criticisms which recur most frequently in Fielding's work probably makes them appear too unoriginal and miscellaneous to form a serious part of a didactic writer's material. But while it is true that Fielding was often repeating strictures previously passed by Steele, Gay, and others, he no doubt felt that he had an ethical justification for doing so. It was the moralist's task to be effective rather than original. Some critics have been puzzled that Fielding should find Dr. South 'wittier than Congreve'; but he was probably thinking of South's own definition: 'Wit in Divinity is nothing else, but Sacred Truths suitably expressed.'[1] Fielding shared this belief in the importance of apt new formulations of familiar ideas. He suggests as much in *An Essay on the Knowledge of the Characters of Men*:

> Neither will the reader, I hope, be offended, if he should here find no observations entirely new to him. Nothing can be plainer, or more known, than the general rules of morality, and yet thousands of men are thought well employed in reviving our remembrance, and enforcing our practice of them.[2]

Since the specific social evils he was concerned to criticize flourished throughout his life it is not surprising to find the same particular targets attacked again and again.

More notable in its effect on Fielding's work is the miscellaneousness of much of his satire. His didacticism tends to take two distinctive forms. The positive side, the propagation of the ideal of Charity, provides a constant point of reference, even when left tacit and only implied through irony. The negative side, the condemnation of various vices, and more particularly of various social practices, finds expression in a host of self-contained, usually satirical, attacks.

---

[1] *Thirty Six Sermons and Discourses*, ed. cit., ii.14.
[2] Henley ed., xiv.283.

It is the heterogeneousness of these attacks which is the other main factor conditioning Fielding's chosen literary forms. As the ensuing chapters will show, the multiplicity of minor didactic comment has a marked effect on the coherence and the continuity of both his dramatic and his narrative writing.

3

Since the corruptness Fielding censured extended to the political and legal administration of the times his satire naturally tended to imply flaws in the system. In his later years, when working as a magistrate, he criticized various specific weaknesses in the law. Yet it never occurs to him to question the system as a whole. He has complete faith in the current social order, and attributes any failings in it solely to the corruptness or inadequacy of individuals. For him any malaise in society can be no more than the sum total of its symptoms.

This implicit confidence in the existing order of things has a special significance for Fielding's didactic position in that he derives from it certain assumptions which do not quite square with his moral beliefs. The slight contradiction involved may be observed in some of his comments on rank. In *An Essay on Conversation* he states: 'Men are superior to each other in this our country by title, by birth, by rank in profession, and by age . . . '[1] Later in the essay he confirms his belief in birth, saying that he would not withhold from it 'that deference which the policy of government hath assigned it'.[2] But at another point he admits:

. . . birth . . . is a poor and mean pretence to honour, when supported with no other. Persons who have no better claim to superiority, should be ashamed of this; they are really a disgrace to those very ancestors from whom they would derive their pride . . . [3]

There is clearly a clash here between Fielding's acceptance of the idea that birth can confer social superiority and his practical view that superiority must depend on some kind of

[1] Henley ed., xiv.257-8.　　[2] Henley ed., xiv.266.
[3] Henley ed., xiv.265.

3—T.R.

intrinsic merit. Elsewhere his position becomes still less certain: 'The respect paid to men on account of their titles is paid at least to the supposal of their superior virtues and abilities, or it is paid to nothing.'[1] Since 'superior virtues and abilities' would be entitled to respect in any case, Fielding implies that title *per se* is a meaningless distinction.

The inconsistency to which he is tending may seem a small one, but its implications are far-reaching. In a sense his dilemma is a product of the basic intellectual ambiguity mentioned at the beginning of this chapter. Reason was made the ultimate criterion, but old forms of thought were still instinctively preserved. Hence in this case Fielding retains his belief in the validity of rank, though he can neither justify it in practical terms, nor derive it from supernatural dispensation.

The effect of this kind of uncertainty is to impair the objectivity essential to his role as moral commentator. For example in both *An Inquiry into the Causes of the Late Increase in Robbers* and *A Proposal for Making an Effectual Provision for the Poor*, he draws a distinction between the idle rich man and the idle beggar. The former is a useful member of the community because his very luxury provides employment and promotes the circulation of money. The latter, however, having only his labour to offer to society, is a useless member, and must legally be compelled to work. Similarly the rich are to be allowed their trivial entertainments, 'their masquerades and ridottos; their assemblies, drums, routs, riots, and hurricanes',[2] while the poor are to be debarred them, since in their case such pleasures are likely to lead to crime: 'In diversions, as in many other particulars, the upper part of life is distinguished from the lower.'[3] When Fielding is discussing the dispensation of charity in *The Champion*,[4] he at once excludes beggars from any benefit, because these 'deserve punishment more than relief'. The chief beneficiaries should be gentlefolk who have impoverished themselves through over-spending.

---

[1] *An Essay on Nothing*, Henley ed., xiv.316.
[2] *Inquiry*, Henley ed., xiii.27.   [3] *Inquiry*, Henley ed., xiii.28.
[4] Henley ed., xv.203 ff.

In all these cases, granted Fielding's confidence in the social system as a whole, his conclusions are very sound; but he has reached them at the expense of introducing an extra-moral premise into what he assumes to be a purely Christian theory of life. Moreover the very system he endorses he is constantly convicting of corruption in practice. Throughout his work, therefore, he is liable to make attacks on the workings of society which cut deeper than he realizes, or to preach absolute moral attitudes which his social preconceptions make it impossible for him to sustain. Where the novels falter it is often due to the fact that though they are didactic works concerned with social morality, the moral and social views of their author are slightly at odds.

III

DIDACTICISM IN FIELDING'S PLAYS

IT seems dangerous, at first sight, to generalize about Fielding's dramatic work, since in his busy theatrical career he wrote not only several kinds of comedy, but also farce, ballad-operas, burlesques, and rehearsal plays. But the diversity is more apparent than real. Fielding's work reflects an Augustan tendency to intermingle the various genres. As Allardyce Nicoll points out: 'Even his best plays show the power of diverse schools—manners, intrigue, humours and sentiment meeting in one.'[1] What is significant, therefore, to a consideration of the forms Fielding had to deal with, is not the particular demands of each individual category, but rather the important factors common to all.

The several current types of comedy were characterized above all by artificiality. Plots were compounded of coincidence, deception, impersonation, and 'discovery'. The leading characters were aristocrats, miraculously freed of any concerns irrelevant to the courtship or intrigue in hand. Their dialogue was epigrammatic in ordinary exchanges, stiltedly emotional in romantic scenes.

But whereas Wycherley, for instance, had exorcized almost every distracting suggestion of real-life emotion or real-life morality, his successors had begun to reinfuse these elements into the artificial context. The sentiment which Steele and Cibber introduced into their plays had automatically a moral implication. Easy's promiscuities, in *The Careless Husband*, cannot be treated as comic once the Steinkirk scene has demonstrated his wife's devotion to him.

Yet *The Careless Husband* illustrates the incompatibility of Cibber's comic and serious intentions. As Bateson comments: 'The fundamental confusion remains; it was beyond Cibber's power to reconcile the artificial values of the

[1] *A History of English Drama 1660–1900*, Cambridge, 1955, ii.158.

Restoration comedies and the ethics of "sentimentalism".[1] In many plays of the period this duality of motive is blatant. For every true drama of sentiment there are several basically immoral comedies brought to a pious conclusion by an unlikely conversion.[2]

The Augustan comic dramatist, however, did not invoke ethical judgements only with respect to the conduct of his chief characters. A certain amount of general social criticism was filtering into the drama. In Mrs. Centlivre's *The Gamester*, for instance, there is a significant little scene in which the hero, for once in funds, lies his way out of paying a long-standing debt to a tradesman who needs the money for his wife's lying-in.[3] John Gay's *The What D'Ye Call It* contains an episode in which three country justices are haunted by the ghosts of five people they have wronged. Primarily it is a parody of the Shakespearean ghost-scene, but the spirits' accusations have a realistic flavour:

> I was begot before my mother married,
> Who whipt by you, of me poor child miscarried.[4]

Where the moralizing grows more serious, however, the limitations of the mixed genre become apparent. Steele's *The Conscious Lovers* is quite heavily didactic; it was avowedly written to attack the practice of duelling,[5] and it contains a number of moral reflections, such as Isabella's dictum on men: 'They have usurped an exemption from shame for any baseness, any cruelty towards us. They embrace without love; they make vows without conscience of obligation; they are partners, nay, seducers to the crime, wherein they pretend to be less guilty.'[6] Yet although the play is ethically relevant to everyday life, its plot depends on several wildly romantic improbabilities, and its dialogue is often lavishly melodramatic: 'No, 'twas Heaven's high will I should be such; to be plundered in my cradle! tossed on the seas!

---

[1] F. W. Bateson, *English Comic Drama 1700–1750*, Oxford, 1929, p. 26.
[2] See Nicoll, *A History of English Drama*, ii.183–4 ff.
[3] 4th ed., London, 1734, p. 33.
[4] *The Poetical Works of John Gay*, ed. G. C. Faber, p. 348.
[5] *Richard Steele*, Mermaid Series, London, 1894, p. 269 f.
[6] Ibid., p. 303.

and even there an infant captive! to lose my mother, hear but of my father! to be adopted! lose my adopter! then plunged again into worse calamities!'¹ The structure and style of the comedy, that is to say, are too formalized for its simple ethical content.

The comedy form which Fielding was to use, then, had already been a vehicle for moral comment; but it was clearly an unsuitable didactic medium for two reasons. First it was essentially an amoral form, at least as far as sex was concerned. Secondly its technique, both of plot and of diction, was too artificial readily to embody moral ideas concerned with the practicalities of ordinary living.

I

Twenty-two of Fielding's twenty-five dramatic works appeared between 1730 and 1737. In 1732 alone he staged five new plays and had a hand in a sixth, one of these, *The Mock Doctor*, being written and produced in three weeks.² Fielding had to make money from an unpredictable audience, and his work was conditioned by their reactions: *The Mock Doctor* was completed in such haste in order to fill the gap in the repertory left by the failure of *The Covent-Garden Tragedy*. Not only was Fielding compelled to write plays fast and frequently: he often found it necessary to adapt them during their run, expanding a success or cutting a failure. A well-known player such as Mrs. Clive might have a part created or enlarged for her. Topical references, social and political, were introduced to gain easy laughs.

It would therefore be pointless to expect too much of the plays: there were obvious commercial reasons why they should be inferior. The brief period in which Fielding could turn out a play contrasts strongly with the 'thousands of hours' he claims to have spent in the composition of *Tom Jones*.³ Nonetheless he asserts in the Prologue to *The Modern Husband* that the Stage:

> ... was not for low farce designed,
> But to divert, instruct, and mend mankind.⁴

¹ *Richard Steele*, Mermaid Series, London, 1894, p. 354–5.
² See Cross, i.129–31.   ³ Henley ed., iv.246.   ⁴ Henley ed., x.10.

and he often claims that his plays have a moral purpose.[1]
Such claims, of course, were a literary commonplace of the
time. How far they had real justification in Fielding's work
can be shown by an examination of *The Temple Beau*, which
provides a good example of the way in which Fielding's
dramatic writing was genuinely modified by a didactic intention.

Allardyce Nicoll classes *The Temple Beau* as a comedy of
intrigue. Certainly part of the play stems from this tradition.
Wilding, the thriftless law-student of the title, conducts
simultaneous affairs with two sisters, one of them married,
surviving a succession of imminent exposures through
desperate resourcefulness. Yet the characterization in the
play derives largely from the Comedy of Humours. Wilding's lovers, Lady Lucy Pedant and Lady Gravely, are
types, respectively, of coquette and prude. Young Pedant,
and his father Sir Avarice, as their names imply, are also
Jonsonian personifications. Fielding, as often, was mixing
two kinds of artificial comedy.

There is a sub-plot, however, which belongs to neither
genre. It tells how Veromil wins Bellaria, Lady Lucy's
niece, despite the treacherous rivalry of his friend Valentine,
who is already engaged to Clarissa. It is a serious story,
seriously treated; none of the three main characters is a
type, nor are they concerned in intrigue.

This need not have meant more than that Fielding wanted
to instil some romantic interest into his play: the various
lovers could have described a sentimental, as the intriguers a
frivolous, pattern. But clearly Fielding is aiming at more than
this, for he involves Bellaria and the rest in a number of
direct conflicts. There is a scene where Veromil persuades
Valentine to put friendship before his lust for Bellaria,[2] and
another where Bellaria forces her lover to believe her
protestations of innocence at the expense of his trust in
Valentine.[3] In what is admittedly a clumsy way, Fielding
causes his characters to face moral decisions. Characterization,

---

[1] Cf. the Prologues to *Love in Several Masques* (Henley ed., viii.11), and
The Coffee-House Politician (Henley ed., ix.75), and the dedication to *Don
Quixote in England* (Henley ed., xi.7).

[2] Henley ed., viii.162 ff.   [3] Henley ed., viii.148 ff.

motivation, and dialogue are on a different level from that of the main plot.

The difference might have remained largely implicit, the worthy behaviour and rather solemn speech of Veromil and Bellaria not being sufficient of themselves to impair the unity of the play. Fielding, however, makes these characters explicitly condemn vice and extol virtue. Veromil, for instance, assures a repentant Valentine: 'The innocent, the perfect joy that flows from the reflection of a virtuous deed far surpasses all the trifling momentary raptures that are obtained by guilt.'[1] This is a straight expression of the latitudinarian idea of 'laudable epicureanism'. When Valentine is tempted, his friend challenges him: ' . . . would you sacrifice our long, our tender friendship, to the faint, transitory pleasures of a brutal appetite? for love that is not mutual is no more.'[2] Such pronouncements disclaim the cheerful amorality which makes Wilding an acceptable and even likeable figure: the play becomes slightly at odds with itself. Yet the disparity between romantic and comic plots need not have been drastic had the moralizing been merely the by-product of the serious situation. Much of the sententiousness, however, far exceeds the scope of the immediate context. It is for no obvious personal reason that Bellaria condemns the fashionable sexual code: 'Inconstancy, which damns a woman, is no crime in man. The practised libertine, who seduces poor, unskilful, thoughtless virgins is applauded, while they must suffer endless infamy and shame.'[3] Veromil, with almost equal inconsequence, denounces the age at large:

> Surprised at villainy, now-a-days! No, Valentine, be surprised when you see a man honest; when you find that man whom gold will not transform into a knave, I will believe it possible you may find that stone which will change every thing into gold.[4]

Not only, then, has Fielding strained the framework of his play by introducing a serious sub-plot, with the discordantly realistic morality which that entails: he has made the

---

[1] Henley ed., viii.164.   [2] Henley ed., viii.163–4.
[3] Henley ed., viii.149.   [4] Henley ed., viii.145.

characters in it mouthpieces for some of his own social and
moral views. Yet he never suggests that the ethics of the
romantic plot should cross-refer to the comic plot. Veromil's virtue is rewarded by Bellaria's hand and the restoration
of his rightful inheritance; but equally Wilding, cheerfully
unregenerate, not only lives to intrigue another day, but
extorts a five-hundred-pound annuity from his father.

In short *The Temple Beau* represents the inconsistencies
typical of the moralizing comedy of the period. What is
unusual is the number and severity of its strictures; Fielding
is at least as critical of society as Steele. Veromil, like Bevil
in *The Conscious Lovers*, rejects a challenge to a duel;[1]
but he also indicts the whole fashionable conception of
honour—'Just the reverse of Christianity'[2]—and on
occasion attacks the general shallowness of the age: 'Virtue
may indeed be unfashionable in this age; for ignorance and
vice will always live together. And sure the world is come to
that height of folly and ignorance, posterity may call this
the Leaden Age.'[3] *The Temple Beau* is particularly significant
of Fielding's didactic intention in that it was only the second
of his plays to be performed. Right at the beginning of his
dramatic career he was prepared to introduce a number of
moral ideas into his work, and they were substantially the
same ideas as he was to advance in his journalism nearly ten
years later.

2

Not all Fielding's plays contain as much ethical material
as *The Temple Beau*, but all include a certain amount. Farce
and artificial comedy give him little scope for recommending
his positive ideals of beneficence, but a good deal for attacking the manners and morals of society. In his first play,
Love in Several Masques, the hero talks of the Town as:
' . . . that worst of wildernesses! where follies spread like
thorns; where men act the part of tigers, and women of
crocodiles; where vice lords it like a lion . . . '[4] Even in
amoral comedies such as *The Letter-Writers* and *The*

[1] Henley ed., viii.163.   [2] Henley ed., viii.131.
[3] Henley ed., viii.131.   [4] Henley ed., viii.63.

Universal Gallant there tends to be criticism of fashionable life. Fielding follows a current trend in genteel comedy by infusing into the portrayals of beaux and courtiers, prudes and coquettes, who figure in these plays, an element of serious satire. The diversions of the Town also come in for slighting comment: in *The Modern Husband*, one of the harshest plays, virtually a whole scene is devoted to an attack on cardplaying.[1]

Above all, however, Fielding censures the venality of fashionable marriage dealings. In *Love in Several Masques* he makes Merital remark: 'In short, beauty is now considered as a qualification only for a mistress, and fortune for a wife',[2] and the point is made again frequently in his later plays. He also suggests some of the results of basing marriage solely on money. Sir Apish Simple, for instance, assures his unwilling bride: ' . . . I'll engage we shall hate one another with as much good-breeding as any couple under the sun',[3] while Lady Lucy Pedant inquires of her niece: 'And have you the assurance to own yourself in love, in an age, when 'tis as immodest to love before marriage, as 'tis unfashionable to love after it?'[4] Fielding's plays depict a number of such 'fashionable' marriages, thriving on mutual detestation. The natural corollary, he demonstrates, is that adultery has become taken for granted. He makes the point even in the farce *An Old Man taught Wisdom*, where the naïve Lucy asks a suitor:

LUCY: Ah, but there is one thing though—an't we to lie together?
BLISTER: A fortnight, no longer.
LUCY: A fortnight! That's a long time: but it will be over.
BLISTER: Ay, and then you may have any one else.[5]

Fielding exposes, in *The Modern Husband*, a particularly unpleasant way in which society marriage was being made a source of income: needy husbands sometimes prostituted their wives to rich lords. Bellamant, the hero of the play, sums up the contemporary situation: 'It is a stock-jobbing age, every thing has its price; marriage is traffic throughout;

---

[1] Act III, scene vi. Henley ed., x.50–51.
[2] Henley ed., viii.25.   [3] Henley ed., viii.81.
[4] Henley ed., viii.124.   [5] Henley ed., x.335.

as most of us bargain to be husbands, so some of us bargain to be cuckolds . . . '[1] The practice condemned in *The Modern Husband*, then, is only an unusually gross example of the general corruptness.

The tendentious comment in the plays, however, is not limited to the concerns of the Town. In *The Author's Farce*, *Pasquin*, and *The Historical Register* there is literary and theatrical satire. Avarice is a frequent subject of attack, most notably in *The Temple Beau* and, of course, *The Miser*. The medical and legal professions earn a spate of incidental jibes:

> Mongst doctors and lawyers some good ones are found;
> But, alas! they are rare as the ten thousand pound.[2]

runs a chorus in *The Lottery*. In *The Coffee-House Politician*, a play bordering on farce, there is a good deal of serious criticism of the law. The villain of the piece, Justice Squeezum, is shown rigging juries and taking protection money from brothels; he warns a prisoner: 'Well, sir, if you cannot pay for your transgressions like the rich, you must suffer for them like the poor.'[3] Worthy's indignation in the last act reflects the underlying earnestness of the play:

> . . . by Heaven it shocks me; that we, who boast as wholesome laws as any kingdom upon earth, should, by the roguery of some of their executors, lose all their benefit. I long to see the time when here, as in Holland, the traveller may walk unmolested, and carry his riches openly with him.[4]

It would be superfluous to try to list here all the topics on which Fielding comments didactically in his drama; as the last chapter suggested, they are too many and too heterogeneous. Only three of the plays embody an overall didactic theme: *Don Quixote in England*, *The Modern Husband*, and *The Fathers*. Don Quixote is made a mechanism for condemning a series of evils: arranged marriages, the tyranny of country squires, and election bribery. The moral purpose of the play is made clear by Fielding's prefatory letter: ' . . . I fancy a lively representation of the calamities brought on a country by general corruption might have a very sensible

---

[1] Henley ed., x.35.   [2] Henley ed., viii.296.
[3] Henley ed., ix.104.   [4] Henley ed., ix.146.

and useful effect on the spectators.'[1] *The Modern Husband* not only anatomizes the current state of matrimony in society, but also makes a calculated attack on the law of criminal conversation.[2] *The Fathers* is a study in contrasted ways of bringing up children, and, as the sub-title implies, an examination of Good-nature. In all the other plays the didactic elements, though recurrent, remain scattered and largely disconnected.

The quality of this didacticism is not particularly remarkable; very often, especially in his attacks on doctors, lawyers, and politicians, Fielding is merely restating contemporary commonplaces. What is significant is the ubiquity of his moral comment and its consequent effect on his form.

Much of it is absorbed conveniently into the text; into the songs, for instance, of *The Author's Farce*:

> The lawyer, with a face demure,
> Hangs him who steals your pelf;
> Because the good man can endure
> No robber but himself.[3]

This is the social paradox which *The Beggar's Opera* had helped to make familiar; although it is close enough to Fielding's general attitude, the idea is expressed too conventionally to be disturbing. Equally such observations can merge satirically into the dialogue. When Constant is under arrest in *The Coffee-House Politician*, Staff brings in a second prisoner, and announces his crime: 'A rape, Captain, a rape —no dishonourable offence—I would not have brought any scoundrels into your honour's company; but rape and murder no gentleman need be ashamed of; and this is an honest brother ravisher . . . '[4] Much of Fielding's didacticism, however, is bluntly imposed on an alien context. In *The Modern Husband*, for example, a Captain Merit appears at Lord Richly's levee, reluctantly compelled to plead for preferment: 'Shall I, who have spent my youth and health in my country's service, be forced by such mean vassalage to

---

[1] Henley ed., xi.7.
[2] See C. B. Woods, 'Notes on Three of Fielding's Plays', *PMLA*, 52 (1937), 359 ff.
[3] Henley ed., viii.245.   [4] Henley ed., ix.111.

defend my old age from cold and hunger, while every painted butterfly wantons in the sunshine?'[1] Having voiced his protests he disappears from the action, his only function being to state Fielding's views about the injustice of the current system of military promotions and rewards. In the same play Fielding devotes a whole scene to satirizing the fashionable enthusiasm for Italian opera,[2] and another (mentioned above) to attacking the vogue for cards.

One more example of Fielding's didactic intrusiveness may be quoted as especially revealing. In *The Grub-Street Opera* Owen Apshinken, an effeminate beau, is bent on seducing Molly Apshones, the daughter of one of his father's tenants. Mr. Apshones assures his daughter that Owen has no honourable intentions, and makes the usual Fielding generalization: 'Poor girl! how ignorant she is of the world; but little she knows that no qualities can make amends for the want of fortune, and that fortune makes a sufficient amends for the want of every good quality.'[3] Later he assails young Apshinken himself:

I desire not, Mr. Owen, that you would marry my daughter; I had rather see her married to one of her own degree.—I had rather have a set of fine healthy grandchildren ask me blessing, than a poor puny breed of half-begotten brats—that inherit the diseases as well as the titles of their parents.[4]

He continues in this full-blooded idiom to the end of the scene, concluding his final speech: ' . . . and if you should prevail on her to her ruin, be assured your father's estate should not secure you from my revenge.—You should find that the true spirit of English liberty acknowledges no superior equal to oppression.'[5] Yet the wretched Owen has been shown in his first speech to be no great menace: ' . . . when once a woman knows what's what, she knows too much for me.—Sure never man was so put to it in his amours— for I do not care to venture on a woman after another, nor does any woman care for me twice.'[6] Apshones's vehement denunciation is wasted on so ineffectual a seducer. In any

[1] Henley ed., x.20. [2] Act III, scene ii. Henley ed., x.46.
[3] Henley ed., ix.236. [4] Henley ed., ix.250.
[5] Henley ed., ix.251. [6] Henley ed., ix.216.

case Owen, rebuffed by the two servant-maids he attempts, ends by marrying Molly. Not only, therefore, do the two scenes in which Apshones appears run counter to the light mood of the ballad-opera, they are quite irrelevant to the plot.

What is more, it seems certain that in the original version of the piece (entitled *The Welsh Opera*) Apshones did not appear at all.[1] This is a clear case of Fielding inserting didactic scenes for their own sake, regardless of their irrelevance to the play as a whole.

Fielding worked over, and added to, many of his plays. *Tom Thumb* went through a series of versions; *Don Quixote in England* and *The Wedding Day* were both refurbished after an interval of years. It was not only in the case of *The Grub-Street Opera* that the additions were didactic. One of his most trenchant attacks on contemporary social standards is an insertion in *The Author's Farce*:

What does the soldier or physician thrive by, but slaughter? The lawyer, but by quarrels? The courtier, but by taxes? The poet, but by flattery? I know none that thrive by profiting mankind, but the husbandman and the merchant: the one gives you the fruit of your own soil, the other brings you those from abroad; and yet these are represented as mean and mechanical, and the others as honourable and glorious.[2]

Fielding's willingness to adapt and enlarge his plays suggests that form was not very important to him. Certainly his

---

[1] The play went through three versions. It was first acted on 22 April 1731, as *The Welsh Opera*. From 19 May it was performed 'with several alterations and additions'. During May Fielding rewrote the piece, expanding it from two to three acts and renaming it *The Grub-Street Opera*. There were also three published versions in 1731. In the first of these (*The Welsh Opera*, two acts) Apshones does not appear. In the second (*The Genuine Grub-Street Opera*, three acts) he has one scene with Owen. The third (Fielding's authorized version, entitled *The Grub-Street Opera*, three acts) allots Apshones a second scene, with Molly. Although the published *Welsh Opera* was denounced by *The Daily Post* as not a true copy (see Cross, i, 111) it seems strong evidence that Apshones's two appearances were among Fielding's extensive additions to the original play.

[2] Henley ed., viii.205. This speech seems to be one of the additions Fielding made when revising the play for production in 1734. It does not appear in the published versions of 1730.

insertion of speeches and episodes solely for their didactic content implies that he subordinated form to his moral intentions. It is not surprising then, to find that his later dramatic work was becoming totally formless. *Pasquin, Tumble-Down Dick, Eurydice, The Historical Register*, and *Eurydice Hiss'd*, his last five pieces before the licensing act virtually ended his dramatic career, were all rehearsal plays. Fielding used the genre very freely, breaking it down to such an extent that what he was really writing was a species of revue, in which all kinds of moral, social, and political points might be made. In *The Historical Register*, for example, the auction, the attack on Cibber[1] and the political scenes are all, in effect, self-contained episodes.

The implication is that Fielding was moving towards a construction so loose as to be able to accommodate any incident he needed to make a didactic point. It is a tendency understandable in a writer whose moral concern generates such a miscellany of practical comments, but it clearly has a limiting effect. *Pasquin* and *The Historical Register* are two of the wittier plays, but they are almost totally lacking in continuity of interest. Moreover the fragmentary style they exemplify, while ideal for attacking particular practices, or even particular personalities, cannot embody those of Fielding's ethical ideas which are expressible only in terms of human relationships. He remains a didactic writer in these plays only to the extent that his satire has a serious purpose. In the novels, where he is concerned both 'to recommend goodness and innocence' and to evoke a picture of life sufficiently coherent and realistic to justify his claim to be a 'historian', this inclination towards the self-contained satirical episode was to be, to some extent, a drawback.

3

It was suggested in the preceding chapter that Fielding was essentially a practical moralist, concerned less with moral doctrine as such than with its application in everyday life. That being so, he was at a great disadvantage in working through a medium which was by definition at a remove

---

[1] See Cross, i.212–13.

from reality. Sometimes he solves the problem by implying that the amoral world of his comedy is an accurate representation of London Society; the intriguing and cuckoldom not being wholly insulated from real-life moral standards. Sir Simon, in *The Universal Gallant,* may be a ridiculous figure, but his reaction to his wife's unfaithfulness involves a serious reflection on the morals of the Town: 'A man that robs me of five shillings is a rogue, and to be hanged; but he that robs me of my wife is a fine gentleman, and a man of honour.'[1] This special attitude of Fielding's means that there is a logical connexion between, say, the satirical portraits of prude and coquette in *The Temple Beau,* and the denunciations of fashionable life in the same play. But the element of comic exaggeration in both characterization and action rather smothers the moral implication.

The nature of eighteenth-century society gave Fielding's comedies another potential which he sometimes exploits. The people whose fatuity, immorality, and corruptness he was portraying were also the wielders of power. They could rig elections, grant or withhold preferment; they were above the law. If Fielding had consistently applied his identification of the amoral comedy world with the contemporary society world, he would have been permanently constrained to the deep pessimism he only sometimes shows. Captain Merit looks in disgust at Lord Richly's coterie:

'Sdeath, there's a fellow now—That fellow's father was a pimp; his mother, she turned bawd; and his sister turned whore: you see the consequence. How happy is that country, where pimping and whoring are esteemed public services, and where grandeur and the gallows lie on the same road!'[2]

It was a point Fielding could not afford to make often. If, for didactic purposes, his comedies were sometimes a means of attacking society life, for commercial purposes they had always to be entertaining, and therefore to observe the traditional standards of artificial comedy. The clash of values in *The Temple Beau* is only one example of the anomalies resulting from Fielding's duality of purpose. *The Wedding Day,* another comedy of intrigue, contains a scene in which

---

[1] Henley ed., xi.111.   [2] Henley ed., x.20.

Millamour, the philanderer-in-chief, is won to virtue by
Heartfort, who preaches Fielding's Good-natured brand of
chastity:

My practice, perhaps, is not equal to my theory; but I pretend to sin
with as little mischief as I can to others: and this I can lay my hand on
my heart and affirm, that I never seduced a young woman to her own
ruin, nor a married one to the misery of her husband.

. . . what can be more ridiculous than to make it infamous for women
to grant what it is honourable for us to solicit . . . to make a whore
a scandalous, a whoremaster a reputable appellation![1]

Here the traditional amorality of the genre and Fielding's
real views on sex are in head-on collision. In the same play
there is a character named Mrs. Useful, who is at first
depicted as being in the comic tradition of bawds. Millamour calls her 'the first minister of Venus, the first pleni-
potentiary in affairs of love'.[2] Later he cries: 'Oh, thou dear
creature! suppose I gave thee worlds to reward thee!'[3]
Yet at the end of the play he fiercely condemns her:

Thou art a more mischievous animal than a serpent; and the man or
woman who admits one of thy detestable character into his house or
acquaintance, acts more foolishly than he who admits a serpent into
his bosom. A public mark of infamy should be set on every such wretch,
that we might shun them as a contagion.[4]

So complete a volte-face demands a selective moral judgement which will condemn Mrs. Useful, but not act retro-
spectively against Millamour himself.

It was suggested at the beginning of this chapter that
fifth-act conversions were fairly frequent in Augustan
comedy. Usually, however, they were simply a convenient
rounding-off device, by which the rake was abruptly re-
formed in the interests of a happy ending. Fielding condemns the practice in *Tom Jones* (book viii, ch. 1),[5] but, as
The Wedding Day shows, was prepared to go much farther
than most of his contemporaries towards attempting to

---

[1] Henley ed., xii.130–1. Heartfort's formulation of Fielding's ideas about
chastity is very similar to that of Tom Jones (book xiv, ch. 4; Henley ed.,
v.108).
[2] Henley ed., xii.72.   [3] Henley ed., xii.78.
[4] Henley ed., xii.139.   [5] Henley ed., iv.65.

introduce a positively reformative element into the intract-
able artificial comedy. Even his lightest works were liable to
be manipulated for this purpose. For instance *Miss Lucy in
Town*, 'a farce with songs', flows along cheerfully as it
shows the bucolic heroine of *An Old Man taught Wisdom*
swiftly acclimatizing herself to city life: ' . . . for if all the
gentlemen in town were in love with me—icod,—with all
my heart, the more the merrier.'[1] But at the end of the play
there is a complete change of mood. Lucy's husband
Thomas, an ex-footman, challenges the lord to whom she has
light-heartedly sold herself: 'I have as good a right to the
little I claim, as the proudest peer hath to his great possessions; and whilst I am able, I will defend it.'[2] He takes
charge of the reluctant Lucy: 'Come, madam, you must
strip yourself of your puppet-show dress, as I will of mine;
they will make you ridiculous in the country, where there is
still something of Old England remaining.'[3] Lucy's father
draws the democratic conclusion: 'Henceforth I will know
no degree, no difference between men, but what the standards of honour and virtue create: the noblest birth without
these is but splendid infamy; and a footman with these
qualities, is a man of honour.'[4] The crux here and elsewhere
is that real-life morality cannot be relevant unless the
characters involved are more realistic than was possible in
artificial comedy. Millamour's conversion and the condemnation of Mrs. Useful only make sense in the light of
ethical standards which would make nonsense of *The
Wedding Day* as a whole. If Thomas's final outbursts are to
be taken seriously Lucy must be seen as not comically but
sinfully frail.

Obviously such sudden shifts of attitude are incongruous,
but even where Fielding tries to be consistently earnest there
is a dissonance. The fact is that there was no machinery for
stage representation of characters real enough to embody
persuasively Fielding's realistic morality. The dialogue, for
instance, was too inflexible. F. W. Bateson remarks: 'It is
one of the curious features of the sentimental comedies of
the eighteenth century that the writing always deteriorates as

---

[1] Henley ed., xii.53.   [2] Henley ed., xii.61.
[3] Henley ed., xii.62.   [4] Henley ed., xii.62–63.

the emotions are intensified.'[1] But it is not, after all, so very curious. The playwrights of the time were using the artificial idiom of the Restoration theatre for their comedies. When they chose to introduce emotional scenes they had to sacrifice the wit which gave that style its effectiveness, and were left with an inexpressively rhetorical mode of speech, lacking any pressure of real feeling. Veromil, in *The Temple Beau*, cries out in the throes of love: 'Eternal transports, agonies of joy delight thy soul. Excellent, charming creature!—But ah! a sudden damp chills all my rising joys; for oh! what dragons must be overcome, before I gather that delicious fruit!'[2] Veromil, however, for all his moralizing, is primarily a romantic character. Bellamant, in *The Modern Husband*, undergoes a much more real conflict, but uses the same stylized manner of address. Torn between his mistress, Mrs. Modern, and the wife he still loves, he soliloquizes at one point:

> What a wretch am I! Have I either honour or gratitude, and can I injure such a woman? How do I injure her! while she perceives no abatement in my passion, she is not injured by its inward decay: nor can I give her a secret pain, while she hath no suspicion of my secret pleasures. Have I not found too an equal return of passion in my mistress? Does she not sacrifice more for me than a wife can? The gallant is, indeed, indebted for the favours he receives: but the husband pays dearly for what he enjoys. I hope, however, this will be the last hundred pounds I shall be asked to lend. My wife's having this dear note, was as lucky as it was unexpected—Ha!—the same I gave this morning to Mrs. Modern. Amazement! what can this mean?[3]

The ideas in this speech could form the basis of an emotional conflict: Bellamant is balancing the duty he owes his wife against the duty he owes his mistress, trying to convince himself that an unperceived injury is no injury. But there seems little emotion in the soliloquy because the expression is too formal. The conventional exclamations, the rhetorical questions, the neat antitheses are inimical to the kind of feeling the situation seems intended to generate.

The conclusion of the speech points to another aspect of the artificiality which suffuses the play: the devices by means

---

[1] *English Comic Drama 1700–1750*, p. 28.
[2] Henley ed., viii.129.   [3] Henley ed., x.56.

of which Bellamant's conflict is to be dramatized are those of the comedy of intrigue. This stylization of both plot and dialogue is damaging to *The Modern Husband* because Fielding is illustrating certain moral imperatives in the story of the Bellamants, which seem more forceful as the relationship embodying them is made convincing and moving. When this is rendered lifeless by formalism the moral content of the play also droops.

The Fathers represents a similar kind of clash between manner and matter. Since Fielding is comparing, in the play, two opposed methods of bringing up children, much of his effect depends upon the plausibility with which he depicts the relationships within the contrasted families. If the result is distinctly unconvincing, it is only partly because the dialogue is as stilted, and the plot nearly as artificial, as usual. In order to make his point Fielding has reduced most of his leading figures to personifications. Mr. Boncour becomes the type of the good-natured parent, while Valence represents miserly self-interest. The result is that although the characters go through the motions of full relationships, the absence of real-life complexity and ambiguity makes their attitudes almost meaningless. The schematic approach and the realistic are clearly irreconcilable.

Since the basis of the schematic approach here is the technique of personification used in the Comedy of Manners, it seems reasonable to relate the inadequacy of *The Fathers*, too, to the limitations of the contemporary dramatic formula. Bateson writes of the drama of the period: 'Its history is that of the strangling of a tentative, still embryonic realism by an obsolete technique.'[1] He is talking of the crude lighting and stage conditions of the time, but his remark is true in a wider sense. It goes far towards explaining Fielding's comparative failure as a playwright.

[1] *English Comic Drama 1700–1750*, p. 150.

IV

JONATHAN WILDE
AND
A JOURNEY FROM THIS WORLD
TO THE NEXT

Jonathan Wild and *A Journey from this World to the Next*
formed part of the *Miscellanies*, which first appeared on
12 April 1743, more than a year after the publication of
Joseph Andrews. There are good grounds, however, for
supposing that both works were written, at least in part,
before Fielding's first novel.[1] In any case it is convenient to
consider them apart from the novels, since in neither case is
the author concerned, in the sense he was later to be, with
telling a story. *A Journey from this World to the Next* is an
imitation of Lucian's *Dialogues*, and his *True History*;[2]
Jonathan Wild has marked affinities with the popular
criminal biographies of the eighteenth century.[3] In both
cases Fielding's form is non-fictional and extremely tractable.
The two works, however, provide further evidence of the
kind of views Fielding was anxious to communicate, and
suggest how his didactic intention was likely to condition a
narrative form.

I

A Journey from this World to the Next falls naturally into
three parts. In the first of these the 'author' describes his
journey to Elysium and his initial experiences there. In

[1] On this point see *Henry Fielding*, by F. Homes Dudden, Oxford, 1952,
i.445–6 and 483.
[2] See L. R. Lind, 'Lucian and Fielding', *The Classical Weekly*, 29 (1936),
84 ff.
[3] W. R. Irwin describes the genre in *The Making of Jonathan Wild*, New
York, 1941, pp. 81 ff.

the second, rather more than twice as long, Julian the
Apostate gives an account of his various transmigrations.
Finally, in a fragment possibly written by Fielding's sister
Sarah,[1] Anne Boleyn tells her story.

In the opening section Fielding finds occasion to stress
the importance of good works, as against mere professions of
faith and dignity. Minos always makes charity his chief
criterion when judging the writer and his fellow spirits.
After rejecting a duke he is addressed by a shade:

. . . who with fear and trembling begged he might not go to the bottom-
less pit: he said, he hoped Minos would consider, that though he had
gone astray, he had suffered for it, that it was necessity which drove
him to the robbery of eighteen pence, which he had committed, and
for which he was hanged: that he had done some good actions in his
life, that he had supported an aged parent with his labor, that he had
been a very tender husband and a kind father, and that he had ruined
himself by being bail for his friend. At which words the gate opened,
and Minos bid him enter, giving him a slap on the back, as he passed
by him.[2]

Another candidate, who 'had constantly frequented his
church, been a rigid observer of fast-days' and 'never been
once guilty of whoring, drinking, gluttony, or any other
excess', is turned back for disinheriting his son.[3] A poet who
pleads the merit of his plays eventually gains admittance only
because 'he had once lent the whole profits of a benefit
night to a friend'.[4] An honest and industrious family,
'starved to death through poverty', are allowed to enter;
their grave parish priest, a pluralist, is refused because he

---

[1] Fielding comments in a footnote at the beginning of the section (Henley
ed., ii.325): ' . . . this chapter is, in the original, writ in a woman's hand:
and though the observations in it are, I think, as excellent as any of the whole
volume, there seems to be a difference in style between this and the preceding chapters; and as it is the character of a woman which is related, I am
inclined to fancy it was really written by one of that sex.' Fielding appends a
rather similar footnote to a letter in *Joseph Andrews* (Henley ed., i.122), and
critics agree that he is there almost certainly referring to his sister. For further
discussion see Aurélien Digeon, 'Fielding a-t-il écrit le dernier chapitre de
A Voyage from this world to the next?', *Revue Anglo-Americaine*, 1931,
pp. 428 ff.

[2] Henley ed., ii.243.   [3] Henley ed., ii.240-1.   [4] Henley ed., ii.241.

failed to give them help: 'for no man enters that gate without charity'.[1]

This emphasis on benevolence is central to Fielding's beliefs, as Chapter II showed. But the moral outlined in his Introduction to *A Journey from this World to the Next* is a rather different one. He claims there that 'our author' (for the work is alleged to survive only as an abandoned manuscript by an unknown hand):

. . . everywhere teaches this moral, That the greatest and truest happiness which this world affords, is to be found only in the possession of goodness and virtue; a doctrine, which as it is undoubtedly true, so hath it so noble and practical a tendency, that it can never be too often or too strongly inculcated on the minds of men.[2]

This axiom, another of Fielding's basic tenets, is negatively illustrated by the experiences of Julian. In a variety of self-centred and dubiously-virtuous incarnations he never finds contentment. As a miser: ' . . . between my solicitude in contriving schemes to procure money, and my extreme anxiety in preserving it, I never had one moment of ease while awake, nor of quiet when in my sleep.'[3] Yet as a rich heir, wildly extravagant, 'in the midst of plenty I loathed everything'.[4] He finds the role of statesman 'subjected daily to the greatest danger and inquietude, and attended with little pleasure, and less ease'.[5] When a soldier he endures horrors 'not to be described, or perhaps imagined'.[6] Both as a fool and as a poet he pines himself to death, and as an alderman ends his days 'in universal contempt'.[7]

It is significant that though Fielding's chief purpose is to promulgate two of his fundamental moral beliefs, he introduces many of the particular subjects he has already discussed elsewhere. He attacks avarice,[8] the medical profession,[9] arranged marriages,[10] beaux,[11] coquettes,[12] and duelling.[13] Even Julian's account of his experiences as a

---

[1] Henley ed., ii.244. [2] Henley ed., ii.213.
[3] Henley ed., ii.262. [4] Henley ed., ii.266.
[5] Henley ed., ii.304 [6] Henley ed., ii.307.
[7] Henley ed., ii.320. [8] Henley ed. (e.g.), ii.223–4.
[9] Henley ed. (e.g.), ii.219. [10] Henley ed., ii.228.
[11] Henley ed. (e.g.), ii.267. [12] Henley ed., ii.241.
[13] Henley ed., ii.219.

Thracian general is made to contain a reminder of the current corruption in military preferment; the emperor Zeno, Julian relates: ' . . . gave me the command of a cohort, I being then but fifteen years of age; and a little afterwards, before I had even seen an army, preferred me, over the heads of all the old officers, to be a tribune.'[1] Fielding is enabled to introduce such points because his narrative is almost infinitely expandable and adaptable. He can touch on any topic he chooses by invoking a suitable spirit, or allotting to Julian an appropriate incarnation. In fact, like the later rehearsal plays, *A Journey from this World to the Next* is practically formless. Eventually Fielding breaks off, declaring that the rest of the manuscript is missing. By this time, after the long stories of Julian and Anna, the original narrator has been forgotten and all sense of continuity has been lost. On the whole Fielding seems to have used his hybrid form merely as an excuse for assembling a number of his usual didactic themes.

2

Jonathan Wild is a more integrated work than *A Journey from this World to the Next* partly because the biographical formula imposes shape and development; the story has a beginning, a middle, and an end. But equally relevant to this coherence is the fact that the underlying ironic attitude, which equates 'Greatness' with villainy, comprehends a number of moral views which in Fielding's earlier work remain scattered. Ambition, selfishness, hypocrisy, cruelty, and cunning are all subsumed under the term 'Greatness' as used in *Jonathan Wild*. If Walpole is attacked it is as the representative of these various characteristics always condemned by Fielding. With the qualities he most detests conveniently summed up in the character of Wild, and exemplified in his career, Fielding can afford to be singleminded and pursue his case in terms of generalization. If he glances at particular practices, in the course of his main narrative, it is usually only by way of a more detailed application of the comparison that is all the time implied: 'Is not

---

[1] Henley ed., ii.263.

as much art, as many excellent qualities, required to make a pimping porter at a common bawdy-house as would enable a man to prostitute his own or his friend's wife or child?'[1] Most of the time he neglects such specific themes, and lets his contrast of tone and subject-matter speak for itself.

The ethical content of the book, however, is not limited to the moral ideas latent in Fielding's irony. There are two sources of additional and often more positive, statement. One of these, of course, is the account of the Heartfrees. It is in this part of the story that Fielding expresses the positive side of 'the doctrine which I have endeavoured to inculcate in this history', namely that Goodness is more conducive to happiness than is Greatness:

> The same righteous judge [i.e. conscience] always annexes a bitter anxiety to the purchases of guilt, whilst it adds a double sweetness to the enjoyments of innocence and virtue: for fear, which all the wise agree is the most wretched of human evils, is, in some degree, always attending on the former, and never can in any manner molest the happiness of the latter.[2]

This idea involves a set of standards alien to those ironically adopted by Fielding in narrating the exploits of Wild. Heartfree himself, therefore, is made the mouthpiece for the many passages of pure moralizing. For instance, he tells Wild:

> There is one thing the loss of which I should deplore infinitely beyond that of liberty and of life also; I mean that of a good conscience; a blessing which he who possesses can never be thoroughly unhappy; for the bitterest portion of life is by this so sweetened, that it soon becomes palatable; whereas, without it, the most delicate enjoyments quickly lose all their relish, and life itself grows insipid, or rather nauseous, to us.[3]

Elsewhere he persuades himself into a contempt of death in a soliloquy that takes up a whole chapter,[4] and in another harangue to Wild makes explicit one of the moral views implicit in Fielding's irony: ' " . . . to me baseness seems

---

[1] Book i, ch. 5; Henley ed., ii.17.
[2] In the Preface to the *Miscellanies*, Henley ed., xii.244.
[3] Book iii, ch. 5; Henley ed., ii.112.
[4] Book iii, ch. 2; Henley ed., ii. 99 ff.

inconsistent with this rule, OF DOING NO OTHER PERSON AN INJURY FROM ANY MOTIVE OR ON ANY CONSIDERATION WHATEVER. This, sir, is the rule by which I am determined to walk ... "'[1] Such direct statements of ethical doctrine certainly weaken the ironic force of the narrative as a whole. That Fielding should impair the stylistic consistency of his book by inserting them is evidence of the seriousness of his didactic purpose. It is also a reminder that although as a moral commentator his chief talent was for satire, he was also by instinct something of a preacher.

The other source of additional didactic comment in *Jonathan Wild* is the unobtrusive, but regular, introduction, independent of the main narrative, of some of Fielding's favourite topics. The fourth chapter of Book I includes a concise exposition of the system of imprisonment for debt,[2] so often assailed in his writings. The tenth contains an attack on beaux.[3] When in prison, Heartfree quite gratuitously voices to the ordinary the latitudinarian view that a sincere Turk might win salvation.[4] Typically, one of Mrs. Heartfree's helpers during her unlucky journey is a lieutenant described as: ' ... a virtuous and brave fellow, who had been twenty-five years in that post without being able to obtain a ship, and had seen several boys, the bastards of noblemen, put over his head.'[5]

Although *Jonathan Wild* is much tauter in construction than *A Journey from this World to the Next*, then, Fielding contrives to work in a variety of local didactic matter. That he does so is significant both of the importance of the didactic motive in his work, and of his attitude to form.

3

At a deeper level *Jonathan Wild* sheds more light on Fielding's moral position. There is an inconsistency in it which illustrates that clash between his ethical views and

---

[1] Book iii, ch. 10; Henley ed., ii.128.

[2] Henley ed., ii.12.

[3] Ibid., 32–33.

[4] Book iv, ch. 1; Henley ed., ii.144. Parson Adams makes the same suggestion in *Joseph Andrews* (book i, ch. 17; Henley ed., i.96).

[5] Book iv, ch. 7; Henley ed., ii.171.

his social preconceptions outlined in Chapter II. Since this discrepancy derives from the inclusion of the Heartfree chapters, it is worth recalling Digeon's plausible suggestion that these were an insertion into an original version which was unremittingly ironic.[1] None the less, whatever the processes of composition, Fielding's final judgement sanctioned a work which combines a ferociously satirical narrative with a bourgeois romance of married life.

In the satirical portion of the book Fielding's method is ironically to approve and recommend all the anti-social attitudes which a gang-leader is likely to have in common with a dictator. The procedure involves, of course, the tacit endorsement of the public-spirited viewpoint which is apparently decried. Naturally the satire gains in scope and power when the moral positions concerned are absolutes, and the irony is unimpaired by the need for qualification.

The most successful parts of *Jonathan Wild* derive authority from just such a lack of compromise. In some of the most striking passages in the book, Fielding shows Wild's philosophy to be a rationalization of the conduct of society's leaders:

'Is not the battle gained by the sweat and danger of the common soldier? Are not the honor and fruits of the victory the general's who laid the scheme? Is not the house built by the labor of the carpenter and the bricklayer? Is it not built for the profit only of the architect and for the use of the inhabitant, who could not easily have placed one brick upon another? ... Cast your eye abroad, and see who is it lives in the most magnificent buildings, feasts his palate with the most luxurious dainties, his eyes with the most beautiful sculptures and delicate paintings, and clothes himself in the finest and richest apparel; and tell me if all these do not fall to his lot who had not any the least share in producing all these conveniences, nor the least ability to do so?'[2]

Much of the book's point derives from the fact that Wild's immoral creed is founded on his accurate observation of various existing social practices. Fielding is condemning any custom or institution which he makes his hero use as a precedent. Here his absolutism has betrayed him into an

---

[1] A. Digeon, *The Novels of Fielding*, London, 1925, pp. 115 ff.
[2] Book i, ch. 8, Henley ed., ii.26–27.

unlikely premonition of Marxism; he is implying a fundamental criticism of the existing social system, which he
would not dream of advancing in practical terms.

If *Jonathan Wild* were purely a work of irony, Fielding's
implied denunciation of capitalism might serve, as it was
presumably intended to do, merely as a convenient moral
reference point. But thanks to the Heartfree chapters the
existing context is too uncertain to accommodate it.

Wild has ironically been shown to be a 'Great Man', in
that, like the corrupt political leader, he takes advantage of
a fallible system. Clearly the system itself is to some extent
condemned. Yet Heartfree, who has been introduced into the
book to represent the positive values which the narrator
purports to scoff at, though appropriately Wild's antithesis
in private morality, founds his life on the same system which
has produced Wild and is exploited by him. In the romantic
part of the book the moral values of the system remain un-
questioned—the emphasis is restricted to the moral values of
the individual. Since Fielding has apparently elected to
affirm his own views as well as to attack false ones, his failure
to state how far he does support the system leaves the criticisms implied in Wild's speech unanswered.

Moreover the Heartfree section further emphasizes the
weaknesses of the existing regime. As Arnold Kettle (who
has admittedly a Marxist axe to grind) shrewdly points out,[1]
Heartfree is quite passive and defenceless in face of Wild's
implacable treachery. When his happiness, and even, it seems,
his life, have been destroyed by Wild, he is obliged to retreat
into religious consolation. Only sheer chance brings redress.
The social order which Heartfree accepts and Wild manipulates provides no protection, still less reward, for the virtuous.

In one sense the confusion involved is a kind of elabora-
tion of that in *The Temple Beau*, where Fielding's sound
workaday morality cast a harsh light on the code of artificial
comedy. In *Jonathan Wild* this morality is itself exposed, by
the absolute ethical standards implied in Fielding's irony, as
enfeebled by the social system.

No doubt this book reveals a failure of literary judgement.
It is notable that the Heartfree story disturbs its whole

[1] *An Introduction to the English Novel*, London, 1954, p. 49.

ironic focus. Ironically speaking, Wild's zenith should be the peak of his material fortune, when his gang is at its most powerful and his income at its greatest. But from the narrative point of view it has to come when he seems most nearly to have destroyed Heartfree, a negligible achievement by Wild's standards. Again, Mrs. Heartfree's long account of her travels slows down the narrative just when it should be gathering speed in approaching the climax, Wild's death.

The inconsistency in *Jonathan Wild*, however, is not primarily the result of literary misjudgement, but of a defect in Fielding's thought. A Marxist might accuse him of being too timid to draw the conclusion of his social observations. But the point is rather that he has not realized just how fundamental is the variance between the Christian morality he is everywhere concerned to recommend, and the practice, if not the theory, of the current English social system. In the light of the contemporary belief in subordination no doubt Fielding could have worked out his own theoretical reconciliation of the eighteenth-century oligarchic system with Christian precept. But he nowhere establishes the requisite fundamental compromise. The result is that often in his work, as in *Jonathan Wild*, there is an underlying moral uncertainty. Only in *Amelia* does Fielding explicitly face the fact that the society he is living in is infinitely remote from the Christian ideal.

V

THE INFLUENCES BEHIND THE NOVELS

I N his plays and early narratives Fielding was manipulating an existing form in the interests of his didactic intention. When he came to write his first novel the position was changed; he was free to design a new form expressly to embody his moral ideas.

Yet although Fielding regarded himself as 'the founder of a new province of writing', he clearly had certain preconceptions which helped to determine the nature of his novels. Various literary genres offered precedents for plot, characterization, dialogue, and style. Moreover a gradual intermingling of these genres had already produced a number of novels of a kind, both in England and in France. There was, then, no abrupt conflation of forms, but rather a merging. Fielding himself, for all his careful theorizing, is no great innovator.[1] If his novels achieve a particularly balanced synthesis it is less the result of an individual feat of imagination than a combination of learning and experience able to profit from the current fusion of techniques and carry it a stage further.

But even though Fielding is combining existing methods it is hard to trace in his novels examples of indebtedness to individual writers. Just as he was steeped in the thought of his age, so he was steeped in its literary experience. In *Joseph Andrews* he pays tribute to Marivaux, Scarron, and Lesage, but he rarely draws upon them directly. G. E. Parfitt, in a detailed study of the French influence on Fielding, remarks: 'On doit se rappeler que Fielding, plus qu'aucun autre auteur se sert surtout de sa mémoire en

---

[1] In this connexion see A. L. Cooke's 'Fielding and the Writers of Heroic Romance', *PMLA*, 62 (1947), 984 ff. Cooke shows that Fielding's theoretical programme was almost identical with that of the romance-writers he professed to despise.

écrivant ses œuvres, ce qui a comme résultat que l'on a souvent une idée des auteurs qu'il a lus, sans pouvoir la préciser.'[1] *In The Covent-Garden Journal* Fielding claims to have 'formed his Stile' on that of Lucian.[2] Yet L. R. Lind, who explores the relationship, can trace only a few minor correspondences. His view resembles Parfitt's: 'Like all great writers . . . Fielding borrowed much which was completely absorbed into his own work, so that accurate identification of the borrowing is next to impossible.'[3] But even if such 'accurate identifications' must be few, it is helpful to gain some idea of the general influences behind the novels. For although Fielding did not have to invent a new genre from scratch, he did have to assemble a kind of narrative adapted to his purpose. He was rejecting, for instance, both the epistolatory form of Richardson and the autobiographical convention of Marivaux and Lesage.

To gain an insight into the way in which Fielding evolved his form, therefore, it is essential to consider, if necessarily in general terms, what other genres and authors seem to have influenced the novels. The rough divisions to be made in this chapter isolate a few important trends for the sake of definition. In practice these trends overlap, and interact with, a number of others less easily sensed and much less easily traced.

I

It has often been noted that the characters of Fielding's novels derive from the tradition of the Comedy of Humours. Certainly he carries over into the novels the general idea of using a quirk of speech or behaviour to provide both entertainment and a useful identification mark. Slipslop's malapropisms, Partridge's Latin tags, and Mrs. Western's political pronouncements all suggest the dramatist's hand. In some cases it is even possible to find among Fielding's plays

---

[1] *L'Influence Française dans les Œuvres de Fielding*, Paris, 1928, p. 99.
[2] *The Covent-Garden Journal*, ii.50.
[3] L. R. Lind, 'Lucian and Fielding', *The Classical Weekly*, 29 (1936), 84 ff.

the antecedent of a particular character. Sir Harry Wilding in *The Temple Beau*, Squire Badger in *Don Quixote in England*, and Sir Gregory Kennel in *The Fathers* all serve as proto-types for Western. Politic in *The Coffee-House Politician* is a fore-runner of Mrs. Western.

But Fielding's debt to the drama here is even greater than at first appears. In fact he takes from the artificial comedy his entire system of characterization. In a typical comedy of the period the *dramatis personae* consisted of a hero and heroine or two and a group of minor figures. The leading roles would be straight romantic parts, the lesser rules 'humorously' comic. In *Love in Several Masques*, for instance, Fielding's first play, there are six main figures: Wisemore, Merital, and Malvil, together with their eventual brides to be, respectively Lady Matchless, Helena, and Vermilia. The minor characters are Lord Formal, Rattle, and Sir Apish Simple, whose names give some idea of their personalities, Sir Positive Trap, who exemplifies snobbery, and Lady Trap and Catchit, respectively prude and resourceful servant-maid. In practice, then, the doings of the romantic characters in the plays furnished the sustaining interest of the action, the 'happy ending' being the successful outcome of their various love-affairs. The minor characters, on the other hand, served only to provide comedy and carry on the plot.

At least in Fielding's first two novels the balance of characterization is substantially similar. There is a pair of romantic lovers, who dominate the story, and a host of friends, relations and chance acquaintances who occupy the peripheral position of the lesser figures in the comedies.

Without doubt this technique contributes certain valuable qualities to the novels. The numerous minor characterizations, for instance, derive from it their unusual definition and vitality. Moreover the machine-like intricacy of plot largely depends on the absolute predictability of the simplified characters. If Western were capable of reason, or Blifil of remorse, the whole course of *Tom Jones* would have to be different; in this respect, too, the 'humorous' manner supplies clarity of outline. It can also, as in the plays, have a didactic usefulness, the humour being equated with a ruling

passion that can hence be satirized. Thus the immensely touchy Colonel Bath is often ridiculed by Fielding, and through him the whole practice of duelling.

This Jonsonian technique, however, also has its limitations for the narrative writer. In a novel which is partly realistic no character appearing with any frequency can plausibly be limited to a single emotion. Thus Mrs. Western, for example, is made a compendium of several humours. She is not just an amateur of politics but also a woman of society and a Beauty *manquée*; virtually all her actions spring from one of these three sources. Similarly Partridge is given alternative motives of cowardice, inquisitiveness, and superstition. Yet somehow this aggregation of humours does not produce a 'rounded' character, on a plane with, say, Tom. In the plays a figure such as Sir Positive or Sir Apish was not permitted the slightest normality of feeling, and so ceased to exist as a moral agent. The lesser characters in the novels, even those who are not confined to a single reaction, are equally devoid of complexity or power of moral choice. There remains, consequently, an absolute division between major and minor figures.

The result is that there can be no very realistic relationship between a leading character and a lesser one; they exist on different levels. Tom's 'love' for Molly Seagrim is thus instantaneously and totally dissipated when he discovers her to be promiscuous. Altogether the influence of the Comedy of Humours produces a formula of characterization in which the leading figures, theoretically at least, are subject to the emotions and morality of real life, while the minor figures remain stylized, and out of touch with normality. This disparity existed in the plays themselves, of course, but it is greatly heightened by the length and circumstantiality of the novels.

It is not only in characterization, however, that Fielding is indebted to the drama. He uses a number of theatrical devices in the novels. The discoveries of Square and Honour[1] in their hiding-places, for instance, recall the similar predicaments of Wilding in *The Temple Beau* and Rakel in *The*

---

[1] *Tom Jones*, book v, ch. 5, and book xv, ch. 7; Henley ed., iii.226, and v.174.

Letter-Writers.[1] As in Fielding's first play masks are used to further intrigue in two of the novels.[2] Tom Jones and Amelia, like Valentine in *The Temple Beau*, are deprived of an inheritance by a scheming relative.

The latter correspondence suggests a more fundamental relationship between the plays and the novels. It is hardly surprising that a few incidental devices for puzzlement or entertainment should have been borrowed from the drama. What is significant is that Fielding, as his reliance on the malevolent relative implies, should have been obliged to take the plot structure of his 'true histories' from the artificial comedy. In fact there can have been no obvious alternative at the time. Fielding's concern for epic regularity demanded a clearcut action to which the incidents of his story could contribute. The novels had to have a resolution which was not simply the result of marriage (as in *Pamela*) or of death (as in *Don Quixote*). Accordingly Joseph Andrews is saved from the seemingly impossible predicament his poverty has brought upon him, by the discovery of his true parentage. Tom Jones is redeemed into solvency and happiness by the unmasking of Blifil's deceit. Booth and Amelia are restored to fortune by the providential news that a large legacy has been treacherously withheld. In the novels, in fact, as often in the plays, traditional variations on loving, losing, and regaining are finally resolved by a comfortable economic solution.

As in the plays this solution is imposed from without. The problems of Joseph, Tom and Booth all stem from lack of money, yet none of them is given the chance to repair his fortunes by work. The truth is, of course, that except by a good marriage there was no obvious way for a gentleman to make money for himself. All Fielding's heroes, therefore, have to be enriched by Fortune; their destiny is never in their own hands. Once again there is clash between formalism and realism: Fielding can invent characters and incidents to embody realistic moral problems, but he can only develop them within a conventional plot, essentially amoral in its separation of effort and reward.

[1] Henley ed., viii.157 and ix.173.
[2] *Tom Jones*, book xiii, ch. 7; *Amelia*, book x, chs. 2–4; Henley ed., v.61 ff. and vii.185 ff.

Another obvious symptom of Fielding's experience as a dramatist is the extensive use of dialogue in the novels. In *Joseph Andrews*, for example, only eight of the sixty-four chapters are completely lacking in direct speech. Moreover the idiom used is in general that of the contemporary theatre. That is to say that the comic dialogues reveal the element of caricature implicit in the Humours tradition, while the emotional episodes are written in the rhetorical style of the stage sentimental scene. Since the novels depict personal relationships more realistically than do the plays, this mannered speech has to encompass more nuances of feeling than it can comfortably express. Ultimately most of the serious relationships in the novels are impaired by the stylization of the dialogue in scenes of emotional crisis.

Altogether, then, Fielding's experience as a dramatist influenced his narratives to the extent that characterization, plot, and dialogue all derive largely from the artificial comedy. The gain in terms of incidental liveliness and a certain formal discipline is obvious. On the other hand it was this same artificiality of technique which smothered a potential realism in several of the plays, and with it their didactic effectiveness.

2

Professor A. R. Humphreys[1] also ascribes to Fielding's training in the theatre his method of emotional analysis by means of personification—the process used, for instance, in the description of Lady Booby's feelings after she has dismissed Joseph: 'Love became his advocate, and whispered many things in his favor. Honor likewise endeavored to vindicate his crime, and Pity to mitigate his punishment. On the other side, Pride and Revenge spoke as loudly against him.'[2] Yet Marivaux had already used such a device in *Le Paysan Parvenu*: 'But on the other side, this Honour pleaded his Cause in my Heart, which was in a perfect Uproar, whilst Ambition pleaded his . . . Said Honour to me, stand your Ground firm . . . Ambition answer'd all this by

---

[1] In 'Fielding's Irony: Its Methods and Effects', *RES*, 18 (1942), 183 ff.
[2] *Joseph Andrews*, book i, ch. 9; Henley ed., i.55.

only a Word or two . . .'[1] The fact that this kind of emotional analysis had already filtered into the novel, illustrates the difficulty, for the critic of Fielding, of separating a specifically chosen, from an unconsciously accepted, technique. Fielding was familiar with various literary genres and with works involving an intertwining of genres. It was open to him to draw either on sources or on adaptations of these sources. Almost certainly he did both.

It is this ambiguity which discourages an assessment of the kind of help he derived from his familiarity with previous novelists. All that can be demonstrated is that he had a respect for certain writers of this kind, and that he was influenced by certain details of their work.

In *Joseph Andrews* (book iii, ch. 1)[2] he refers respectfully to four writers who might be classified as novelists: Cervantes, Lesage, Scarron, and Marivaux.[3] Since the title-page of the first edition bore the sub-heading 'Written in imitation of the Manner of Cervantes', it might be thought that Fielding had made a large number of specific borrowings from *Don Quixote*. But his debt seems, on the whole, to have been limited to an adaptation of the central formula, much of the substance of his novel consisting of the involuntary exposure of hypocrisy by the quixotically innocent Parson Adams. There are a number of similarities of detail, but these, while suggestive in quantity, are individually trifling.[4]

Lesage's *Gil Blas*, like *Don Quixote*, relates the various adventures of a single vagabond and involves a prolixity of incidents and characters. But its particular influence on

---

[1] *Le Paysan Parvenu* (anonymous translation), London, 1735, 30–31.

[2] Henley ed., i.212–14.

[3] Fielding frequently pays tribute to Cervantes, of course. He praises Marivaux again in *Tom Jones* (book xiii, ch. 1; Henley ed., v.33) and refers to Scarron's *Le Roman Comique* in *The Opposition; A Vision* (Henley ed., xiv.323). *Don Quixote* had been frequently translated, and Fielding's library included a copy of Jarvis's rendering (1749 edn.). Unlike Richardson Fielding could have read the four French novels principally concerned in the original, but in any case *Gil Blas, Le Roman Comique*, and *La Paysan Parvenu* had all been translated by 1735, and *Marianne* was translated in instalments between 1736 and 1742.

[4] Battestin lists a number of these (*The Moral Basis of Fielding's Art*, p. 176).

Fielding seems to have been slight. Scarron, however, made use of at least one specific device later to be found in *Joseph Andrews* and *Tom Jones*: the mock-heroic descriptions of time. *Le Roman Comique* begins:

> Bright Phoebus had already perform'd above half his Career; and his Chariot having past the Meridian, and got on the Declivity of the Sky, roll'd on swifter than he desir'd . . . To speak more like a Man, and in plainer Terms; it was betwixt five and six of the Clock . . . [1]

It is Marivaux, however, who seems to have had the most direct influence on Fielding. Early in *Le Paysan Parvenu* he begs leave to digress:

> . . . for it's proper I should accustom my Readers betimes to my Digressions; I am not very positive whether I shall be guilty of many, perhaps I may, and perhaps I may not; I can answer for neither; only this I am resolv'd, not to confine my self . . . [2]

Fielding claims a similar licence in *Tom Jones*:

> Reader, I think proper, before we proceed any farther together, to acquaint thee that I intend to digress, through this whole history, as often as I see occasion, of which I am myself a better judge than any pitiful critic whatever . . . (book i, ch. 2)[3]

Again, Marivaux's use of the story of the fallen Mlle. du Bois as what Crane would call a 'negative analogy' to Marianne's, is paralleled in *Tom Jones* and *Amelia*, where the histories of Mrs. Fitzpatrick and Mrs. Atkinson show the fates which the respective heroines of these novels might have incurred had they succumbed to weakness. Within such reported stories Fielding often explains an implausible exactness of detail in the kind of terms Marivaux uses: ' . . . I lost not a syllable of what she said; for it made such an impression upon my mind, that, I believe, I have repeated it word for word.'[4]

---

[1] Scarron's *Whole Comical Works* (translated by Brown, Savage and others), London, 1700, p. 1. Compare, for example, *Joseph Andrews*, book i, ch. 8; Henley ed., i.47.

[2] p. 6.

[3] Henley ed., iii.22.

[4] *The Virtuous Orphan; or, the Life of Marianne* (anonymous translation), *The Novelist's Magazine*, 16, London, 1784, p. 15. (This is the earliest

These minor similarities of technique suggest that Fielding was fairly closely acquainted with the work of his Continental predecessors. It seems reasonable to suppose therefore that he derived from them certain broad narrative effects that his novels have in common with theirs. It may be noted, for example, that all the five novels concerned proceed chronologically through a series of brief, intrinsically entertaining, and virtually self-contained episodes. The unifying principle in each case is that the adventures all centre round a single character or group of characters. All five stories range over a wide cross-section of society.

One more particularly significant point is that all four authors use interpolated stories to diversify their main narrative, and in fact show a general willingness to introduce extraneous matter. It is assumed that part of the narrative-writer's business is to keep up a commentary on manners and morals. The common attitude seems to be fairly, if light-heartedly, expressed in Scarron's *Les Hypocrites*, where after a burst of sententiousness he concludes:

> And now methinks I see some malapert Critick cock his Hat, toss his Wig over his Shoulders, look fierce, and ask how these Moral Aphorisms come to be thus brought in hand over head. Why, pray Sir don't be so cholerick; make use of them, or let them alone as you see fit; 'tis all a case to your humble Servant, I'll assure you; but under favour, Sir, methinks you ought to thank the man who gives you them for nothing.[1]

Marivaux and Cervantes go a stage further, and even insert passages of literary theory and criticism.[2] The scope for digression perhaps depends on the fact that all the novelists except Scarron are recounting adventures seen from a distance. The autobiographers are looking back on youthful adventures from a serene middle age; Cervantes appraises

English translation available in the Bodleian Library.) Compare, for example, *Amelia*, book iii, ch. 1; Henley ed., vi.111. Cervantes, however, uses a similar technique.

[1] *The Whole Comical Works*, 'The Hypocrites', p. 70. (Owing to an error in pagination 'The Hypocrites' contains two pages 70. This is the second of them.)

[2] (e.g.) *Don Quixote* (trans. Jarvis), London, 1749, i.372 ff., and *Le Paysan Parvenu*, 262 ff.

Quixote's exploits from an ironic height. In each case the result is a certain disengagement from the action. Marianne may be more deeply committed to stirring the reader's feelings, but even she can always withdraw sufficiently from her past to point a moral, or to generalize about human nature.

As far as tone is concerned, however, Fielding was probably at least as much influenced by his work as a journalist. Like Steele and Addison, of course, he had made his editorials exercises in polite didacticism, and he had often adopted the widespread practice[1] of stating a general ethical premise, illustrating it by an example, and then drawing the moral. A typical *Spectator* essay begins: 'The most improper things we commit in the Conduct of our Lives, we are led into by the Force of Fashion.'[2] Fielding opens many of his articles with a similar kind of generalization: 'The conquest of one's self is justly preferred by wise men to that of armies and kingdoms.'[3] It is not surprising to find him carrying over this aphoristic style into the novels. A chapter in *Joseph Andrews* starts: 'Habit, my good reader, hath so vast a prevalence over the human mind that there is scarce any thing too strange or too strong to be asserted of it' (book iv, ch. 7).[4] The recurrence of this gnomic manner suggests Fielding's didactic concern in the novels. In the above instance, as in many others, he proceeds from his opening statement to an illustrative anecdote which leads into a generalized discussion. Finally the issue is narrowed down to the effect on Lady Booby of a habitual pretended aversion to men. As regularly happens in Fielding's novels, the local incident has been made to point a moral.

The aphoristic habit also helps to fix Fielding's tone as narrator. 'My good reader' is the typical vocative of polite journalism; the authoritative but informal tone of Fielding's occasional essays is also to characterize his manner in the

---

[1] Described by I. Z. Sherwood in 'The Novelists as Commentators', *The Age of Johnson, Essays presented to C. B. Tinker*, New Haven, 1949, pp. 113 ff.

[2] No. 64.

[3] *The Champion*, Henley ed., xv.177.

[4] Henley ed., i.339.

novels. Since the French novelists have a similar approach
to the reader it is impossible to guess whether narrative or
journalistic tradition has the greater influence here. But the
question is hardly worth deciding, because the similarity of
manner in the two genres represents a common attitude to
matter, an attitude which Fielding shares. 'He asks that the
reader should survey life, rather than experience it', comments Kettle.[1] If this is true, however, it is not because
Fielding's detached, well-mannered, generally ironic tone
accidentally discourages the reader from too close an involvement in the action. Style and content both stem from an
assured, objective mind, confident of a capacity to interpret
experience, to derive rules of conduct from it, and to create
incidents and characters which will embody those rules
unambiguously.

Much has been written about the influence of classical
epic on Fielding, but Ian Watt plausibly dismisses such
influence as 'very slight' and 'mainly retrograde', useful
chiefly in setting him an exalted standard.[2] This last point,
however, is more important than Watt seems to suggest.
Without a consciousness of classical precedent the cultivated
Fielding might well have hesitated to involve himself with the
novel at all. And his awareness of tradition provides him with
criteria for scale, variety, and formal discipline. Finally it
has its own effect on Fielding's tone within the novels.

Epic precedent demanded a certain dignity of style and
incident. Since Fielding was writing comedy the heroic
manner would have been incongruous. Like many of the
Augustans he reconciles comedy and dignity by means of a
mock-heroic manner. This is most evident in such totally
stylized scenes as that of Joseph's fight with the hunting-
pack, or the churchyard battle in *Tom Jones*. Elsewhere,
however, this tone is generally diffused. There are mock-
heroic descriptions of time, probably borrowed from Scarron;

[1] *An Introduction to the English Novel*, i.80.
[2] *The Rise of the Novel*, London, 1960, p. 259. In general Watt's summary
seems to me much more realistic than such tortuous investigations as E. M.
Thornbury's *Henry Fielding's Theory of the Comic Prose Epic*. Fielding's
pronouncements about the requirements of prose epic are usually only
grandiose formulations of the current practice of many narrative writers.

Slipslop becomes 'this fair creature', Mrs. Partridge 'this Amazonian heroine', and Tom 'our hero'. The touch of pedantic humour harmonizes both with Fielding's usual ironic tone, and with the formalized dialogue. It helps to reduce personal involvement with character or story to a minimum.

There is one more major influence on Fielding's novels, however, which is almost antithetical to this stylization: his concern with truth to life. Cervantes had suggested the programme in general terms: 'All it [i.e. *Don Quixote*] has to do, is, to copy Nature: Imitation is the business, and how much the more perfect that is, so much the better what is written will be.'[1] Marivaux carries the idea even further; he writes in *Le Paysan Parvenu*: ' . . . this I dare assure the Reader, that the Facts are all really true, it's not a History forg'd for Diversion, which I imagine will easily be discern'd.'[2] In eighteenth-century England Truth to Nature was in any case a conventional literary principle in all genres. Fielding, however, interprets the idea much more narrowly than most of his contemporaries, claiming in his preface to *Joseph Andrews* that:

. . . every thing is copied from the book of nature, and scarce a character or action produced which I have not taken from my own observations and experience, yet I have used the utmost care to obscure the persons by such different circumstances, degrees, and colors, that it will be impossible to guess at them with any degree of certainty . . . [3]

In the last book of *Joseph Andrews* he justifies an extraordinary comment of Didaper's in a footnote: 'Lest this should appear unnatural to some readers, we think proper to acquaint them that it is taken verbatim from very polite conversation' (book iv, ch. 9).[4]

There is evidence at all levels of this realistic bent in Fielding. *Tom Jones* is based on an exact scheme of time and geography, worked out with almanac and map. In common with *Joseph Andrews* it includes some real inns and real innkeepers. Models have been found for certain characters. Parson Adams seems without doubt to have been drawn from the Reverend William Young, and Peter Pounce from

---

[1] *Don Quixote*, book i, Author's Preface, penultimate paragraph.
[2] p. 3. [3] Henley ed., i.24. [4] Henley ed., i.357.

a miserly lawyer named Walter; Fielding admits that the portrait of Sophia is based on his own first wife.[1] Sporadically the dialogue develops a real-life vitality; in the blunt vernacular of Mrs. Tow-wouse's 'Common charity a fart!' for example, or the righteous indignation of Mrs. Miller's ' . . . if any other person had called him villain, I would have thrown all this boiling water in his face'.[2]

The inference seems to be that Fielding saw no discrepancy between the Truth claimed by previous fiction-writers, and the Truth of Life itself. As a result he inserted raw fragments of his personal experience and observation into novels which various other literary influences combined to make formal in plot, characterization, and style.

3

With the exception of this concern for verisimilitude, then, the various literary tendencies mentioned in this chapter are fully compatible with each other. They are also well adapted to at least part of Fielding's didactic intention.

It was suggested earlier that Fielding's later plays resolved into a series of sketches, each one making a distinct moral or social observation. The picaresque formula of the Continental fiction-writers offered him the chance again to disperse his views in self-contained incidents. A concern for classical regularity makes him impose some unity on these incidents by relating them to an artificial plot, and he calls the result a 'Comi-prosai-epic'; but it is essentially a *loose-leaf* epic. Granted a slight functional link with the chain of events composing the action, an episode designed to embody any of Fielding's views could be inserted into his novel. In any case the narrative manner he had adopted gave him scope for a large measure of direct comment. It was even open to him to digress from his story altogether in order to make a point.

In other ways, too, didactic and literary requirements could be identified. The 'flat' minor characters derived from

---

[1] Most of these points are elaborated in the chapters on the individual novels.

[2] *Tom Jones*, book xvii, ch. 2; Henley ed., v.249.

the Comedy of Humours not only added life to the picaresque story but could readily be manipulated into patterns illustrating a didactic view. They could also be made to represent distinct attitudes to be defended or attacked, especially since the stylized idiom of current literary dialogue made elaborate formal statements of moral ideas a possibility. Even the current tone of essayist or narrator was appropriate, in its detachment. Fielding could evaluate for his readers the characters and incidents he created and manipulated, interpreting the patterns he himself imposed.

If this had been the whole story the resulting works must surely have been 'moral fables', such as *Candide* or *Animal Farm*. As the ensuing chapters will show, there are incidents in Fielding's novels which have a comparably schematic quality; but the total effect of the narratives derives to a great extent from their closeness to ordinary human experience. One reason for this has been suggested in this chapter: Fielding's pursuit of Truth to Life leads him to introduce into his novels all kinds of material drawn directly from his personal observation. He could hardly reduce a heroine based on his beloved Charlotte to the status of a Cunégonde.

The other reason has been put forward earlier in this book. Fielding is naturally drawn to realism by the nature of his moral beliefs. What he regarded as vices could be adequately represented by the 'two-dimensional' figures of the tradition of humours, but the 'good' he preached was an everyday charity and sympathy which was not to be so glibly personified. Heartfree and Allworthy, who come closer than any of his other characters to being 'types' of virtue, remain lifeless and insipid. Good-nature can only be felt as real when invested with the human warmth and absurdity of Adams, or the human gaiety and faultiness of Tom Jones. Moreover, since one of Fielding's themes is the contrast in practical results between this positive goodness and the theoretical virtue of the hypocrite, he naturally requires a realistic setting to provide his perspective. It is because Black George's family are shown suffering 'all the misery with which cold, hunger, and nakedness can affect human creatures'[1] that the generosity of Tom, who tries to help

[1] Henley ed., iii.137.

them, and the meanness of Blifil, who tries to prevent him doing so, are vividly realized. Increasingly in his narratives Fielding defines a good or bad action by means of a circumstantial context.

The general conclusion must be that there was a fundamental ambiguity in Fielding's approach to the novel. He was trying to produce work at once formalized and realistic. It is quite remarkable, therefore, that he achieved such comparatively harmonious results. Criticisms levelled against particular limitations in the novels are often an involuntary compliment to the skill with which he had compromised. Those who complain, for instance, that certain characters are 'two-dimensional', or that, say, the episode of Tom's encounter with the gypsies is irrelevant, imply that the characterization in general is realistic, or that most of the episodes which compose *Tom Jones* have been adequately fused into the plot. In other words they are accepting Fielding's form as a consistent whole, with an internal logic abrogated only by certain details. As this chapter has tried to suggest, it was really a conflation of various literary methods into a medium for his didacticism. The surprising thing is that the resulting syntheses should have sufficient breadth, vitality, and consistency to warrant assessment as coherent pictures of eighteenth-century life.

The tension between realism and formalism, however, is not resolved in the same way in all three novels. In each case the emphasis is different, and the component elements are rearranged. As Fielding's didactic intention grows progressively more sophisticated his novels develop in seriousness and complexity.

VI

JOSEPH ANDREWS

Joseph Andrews is not only the shortest of Fielding's novels, but also the simplest in form. Indeed the whole structure of the book can be fairly explained in terms of its three main constituent parts. The story begins as a parody of *Pamela*, develops into an adaptation of Cervantes's picaresque formula, and concludes with the kind of happy ending characteristic of the artificial comedy. It is, moreover, a very light-hearted novel, containing a much greater proportion of pure comedy than *Tom Jones*.

Nonetheless Fielding's literary intention is plainly serious. He claims to be attempting a new kind of writing, the comic prose epic, 'which I do not remember to have seen hitherto attempted in our language' (Preface).[1] Carefully he distinguishes this genre from Romance and Burlesque. He numbers himself with Cervantes, Lesage, Scarron, and Marivaux as a historian, recording fundamental truths about human nature. A book such as *Don Quixote*, he suggests: '... is the history of the world in general, at least that part which is polished by laws, arts, and sciences; and of that from the time it was first polished to this day; nay, and forwards as long as it shall so remain (?)' (book iii, ch. 1).[2] Fielding consequently lays great stress on truth to life, asserting that in *Joseph Andrews* 'every thing is copied from the book of nature, and scarce a character or action produced which I have not taken from my own observations and experience' (Preface).[3]

But in addition to this formal aim Fielding has a moral aim. He is concerned to expose vanity and hypocrisy: '... to hold the glass to thousands in their closets, that they may contemplate their deformity, and endeavour to reduce it, and thus by suffering private mortification may avoid

[1] Henley ed., i.17.   [2] Henley ed., i.214.   [3] Henley ed., i.24.

public shame' (book iii, ch. 1).[1] He reconciles this programme with his new form by making the picaresque adventures embody a succession of the particular attacks on affectation which he had made many times before in his writings. The novel becomes a sequence of didactic episodes, its plot being so loosely knit that Fielding can insert an adventure in dialogue illustrating any idea he chooses.

There remains, however, some conflict between Fielding's literary and didactic intentions in *Joseph Andrews*. His concern to shape his incidents into a series of neat moral comments naturally militates against the realism and continuity of the book. None the less critics have always judged it, like any other novel, in terms of character and plot. Such an approach is clearly inappropriate to a story constructed largely as a sequence of self-contained episodes, contributing to the action only in their narrative concentricity. Digeon, Cross, and Dudden all describe at length the various adventures in which Parson Adams is embroiled, but chiefly for the light these shed on the characterization. In fact it would almost be true to say that Adams is created as a necessary condition of these incidents, rather than that they are invented to illustrate different qualities in him.

This chapter will try to show how far *Joseph Andrews* was designed as a series of didactic episodes, and how far as a picture, arbitrarily stylized, of real life. Finally it will suggest what sort of whole these discordant aims produce.

I

Battestin claims that *Joseph Andrews* shows the specific influence of the latitudinarian homilists. In defining the sum of a Christian's goodness as 'chastity ... with respect to himself, and charity with respect to society', they regularly instanced Joseph as epitomizing the former quality, and Abraham the latter; hence the parallel exemplification in Fielding's novel.[2]

The representation of virtue in *Joseph Andrews* is therefore twofold; and this dichotomy is reflected in the

---

[1] Henley ed., i.214.   [2] *The Moral Basis of Fielding's Art*, pp. 26 ff.

narrative form. In effect the first ten chapters of the first book and much of the last book constitute a romance of which Joseph is the hero, while the rest of the novel comprises a variety of picaresque adventures in which Adams is the central figure. Joseph's story begins, at least, as a parody of *Pamela*; Adams's justifies the book's sub-heading: 'written in imitation of the manner of Cervantes'.

The history of Joseph, however, provides the formal framework for the adventures of the book's long central section, and has consequently to include all the paraphernalia of introduction, plot, and discovery. Even so it occupies less than a third of the novel. Only one important moral point is made: the sincere, uncomplicated relationship between Joseph and Fanny embodies an attitude towards love which is in deliberate contrast to that in *Pamela*. The element of parody dilutes but does not disguise this moral intention. On the whole, however, this part of the book has little bearing on the general didactic purpose.

The substance of *Joseph Andrews*, both quantitatively and thematically, is the account of the journey from London to Adams's parish. Functionally it is independent of the rest of the story. Apart from the encounters with Mr. Wilson and the pedlar, nothing happens on the journey which affects the outcome of the novel. The chapters in question consist of a succession of episodes which are self-contained, but for a certain amount of narrative coupling, and which almost invariably make some moral point. (Those fights and comic dialogues included solely as entertainment are the only exceptions.) When Joseph sets out for home the plot has come to a complete standstill. The ensuing happenings are relevant to this plot only because they delay his arrival.

Perhaps Joseph's first mishap supplies the clearest guide to Fielding's intentions, since with his action at a halt the author is free to exert any kind of fresh impetus he chooses. What he does choose is to retell the parable of the Good Samaritan in contemporary terms. Joseph is robbed and stripped, and his naked body flung into a ditch. A stage-coach stops when the postillion hears his groans, and the passengers debate whether to assist the injured man.

An old gentleman is for hastening away at once, for fear of

a second robbery. A lawyer counsels assistance, but only because he fears the consequences to himself should Joseph die through lack of aid. The only woman occupant of the coach, however, is firmly against admitting a naked man, and in any case the coachman refuses the extra passenger till won over by bribes and threats. Like the travellers and the lady's footman he declines to lend the victim any kind of garment, and it is left to the postillion—'(a lad who hath since been transported for robbing a hen-roost)'—to provide Joseph with a greatcoat.

The author makes Joseph's injuries continue to produce moral repercussions right up to the end of Book I. Not only the reactions of the coach-party are scrutinized, but also those of Mr. Tow-wouse, Mrs. Tow-wouse, Betty, a clergyman, a doctor, and Parson Adams. In all, the goodwill of a dozen people is tested by Joseph's misfortune, in each case with a different and plausible result. The robbery initiates a series of events clearly designed to form an elaborate little commentary on charity and hypocrisy at a variety of social levels.

The extent to which the didactic aim takes priority is underlined by two facts. The episode is self-contained, since not only does Joseph make a complete recovery from his wounds, but the one robber who is captured is allowed to escape, and none of the coach-passengers reappears in the novel. Fielding's manner of narration also makes it quite clear where he wants the emphasis to fall. Joseph's injuries are never described or even specified, and the attack itself is introduced perfunctorily in mid-sentence: 'He had not gone above two miles, charmed with the hope of shortly seeing his beloved Fanny, when he was met by two fellows in a narrow lane, and ordered to stand and deliver' (book i, ch. 12).[1] Joseph is so stylized and idealized a figure that there is no personal involvement in his plight. The robbery and its consequences are interesting not as part of Joseph's story, but for the reactions they evoke from various people.

Within the parable Fielding is able to re-express a number of his stock prejudices. The squeamish woman who looks at the naked Joseph through the sticks of her fan but refuses

[1] Henley ed., i.62.

to allow him in the coach is typical of the hypocritical prudes Fielding constantly satirized. The lawyer and Mrs. Towwouse represent the self-interested Hobbesian philanthropy he detested. The quack who attends Joseph at the inn is of the kind Fielding exposes in *The Mock-Doctor* and elsewhere, and he talks the same jargon: ' "The contusion on his head has perforated the internal membrane of the occiput, and divellicated that radical small minute invisible nerve which coheres to the pericranium ..." ' (book i, ch. 14).[1]

The first episode in *Joseph Andrews* not dependent on the *Pamela* parody, then, shows Fielding resorting to the picaresque pattern of summary incident, but infusing the incident with moral significance. The particular misadventure with which he begins is used to link a group of seven chapters; the subsequent episodes, though briefer, fulfil the same kind of piecemeal didactic purpose. He moulds the adventures of his travellers into a series of short satires which embody many of his views on social morality.

These wayside incidents and dialogues illustrate what Fielding considered to be common attitudes of meanness or hypocrisy. If this were all, *Joseph Andrews* would be no more than a sequence of parables. The separate episodes are linked, however, by the presence of Parson Adams who, in his consistent innocence and humanity, represents Fielding's ideal of Good-nature. Adams's presence gives the novel an obvious advantage in construction over *The Historical Register* or *A Journey from this World to the Next*. In the play the various self-contained points were only perfunctorily linked by the rehearsal plan. Like Fielding's other rehearsal plays it amounts to no more than the sum total of its episodes. *A Journey from this World to the Next* collapses into an even more aimless consecutiveness. In *Joseph Andrews*, however, the adventures have an Odyssean unity in that they all involve one central figure. Moreover this figure, Parson Adams, represents the permanent standard of goodness which exposes the falsity of the hypocrites encountered in his travels.

In short, *Joseph Andrews* provided scope, theoretically at least, for a complete embodiment of Fielding's moral

[1] Henley ed., i.76.

views. The positive side of them could find expression chiefly in the characterization of Parson Adams, the negative side in the attitudes exemplified by various of the people he meets.

A corollary of the method is that the characters of these people must emerge as two-dimensional, since each one represents some moral standpoint. Fielding himself admits as much in the introduction to Book III: ' . . . I describe not men, but manners; not an individual, but a species.'[1]

What the central section of *Joseph Andrews* primarily consists of is Parson Adams's introduction to a series of such semi-allegorical figures, on whom, implicitly or explicitly, he passes judgement. Many of these encounters are very brief and many are entangled with the purely burlesque or purely functional incidents. It would therefore be too intricate a task to trace the whole series of didactic episodes from the beginning of the journey to its end. But a number of examples will illustrate the general method.

Adams hears two vastly different accounts of a certain squire. It transpires that the speakers have been winner and loser of an action decided by the man in question. ' "God forbid!" said Adams, "that men should arrive at such a pitch of wickedness to belie the character of their neighbor from a little private affection, or, what is infinitely worse, a private spite" ' (book ii, ch. 3).[2] After a fight at an inn a stranger slily suggests to Adams that with a little distortion of the facts he might gain legal damages from his opponent:

'How, sir,' says Adams, 'do you take me for a villain, who would prosecute revenge in cold blood, and use unjustifiable means to obtain it? If you knew me, and my order, I should think you affronted both.' (book ii, ch. 5)[3]

Unable to pay his bill at another inn he visits Trulliber, a fellow clergyman, to seek a loan, but is treated with rudeness, and dismissed with a contemptuous refusal. Adams condemns him outright:

'Now, there is no command more express, no duty more frequently enjoined, than charity. Whoever therefore, is void of charity, I make no scruple of pronouncing that he is no Christian.' (book ii, ch. 14)[4]

[1] Henley ed., i.215.   [2] Henley ed., i.114.
[3] Henley ed., i.141.   [4] Henley ed., i.193.

Peter Pounce, Lady Booby's steward, an inveterate miser, suggests to Adams as they are travelling in a coach on the last stage of the journey home, that 'the distresses of mankind are mostly imaginary': '"Sure, sir," replied Adams, "hunger and thirst, cold and nakedness, and other distresses which attend the poor, can never be said to be imaginary evils"' (book iii, ch. 13).[1]

The interpolated stories, and particularly that of Wilson, have the effect of expanding the cross-section of society on which Fielding (usually through Adams) is enabled to comment. Wilson's history is unconvincing as autobiography precisely because it constitutes so full a survey of the vices of London society. First he describes the kind of shallow pursuits which occupied him, and gives the diary of a typical day: 'At which Adams said, with some vehemence, "Sir, this is below the life of an animal hardly above vegetation . . . "' (book iii, ch. 3).[2] Then Wilson tells of his sexual adventures, ranging through affairs with common prostitutes, a kept mistress, a seduced girl, a coquette, and a married woman. Each kind of relationship brings its own punishment—disease, betrayal, remorse, unfulfillment, legal penalties. He admits that finally: '"I looked on all the town harlots with a detestation not easy to be conceived; their persons appeared to me as painted palaces, inhabited by Disease and Death . . . "' (book iii, ch. 3).[3]

The rest of his London career—his encounter with the Rule of Right, his ruin by gambling, his work as a hackwriter—has a similar kind of unlikely comprehensiveness. Once again Fielding is taking the opportunity of making as many different specific points as he can.

Many of these are the customary onslaughts. Wilson's vain pursuit of a coquette is made the occasion for a long attack on the whole class. His predictable imprisonment for debt produces an incredulous outburst from Parson Adams. The seduction of inexperienced girls, so often deplored by Fielding, is here shown carried to its logical conclusion, with the victim, diseased and debauched, ending her days in Newgate. The girl, incidentally, was:

[1] Henley ed., i.310.   [2] Henley ed., i.232.   [3] Henley ed., i.237.

' ... the daughter of a gentleman, who, after having been forty years in the army, and in all the campaigns under the Duke of Marlborough, died a lieutenant on half pay, and had left a widow, with this only child, in very distressed circumstances ... ' (book iii, ch. 3)[1]

Yet another of Fielding's stock social criticisms has been edged into the text.

In other parts of the narrative, too, familiar points are made. Didapper, a character quite extraneous to the action, is introduced into the last book to provide an excuse for Fielding's usual satire against beaux. The practical jokes played on Adams by the hunting squire and his toadies recall the attack on 'roasting' in *The Champion*.[2] Bellarmine and the traveller from Italy show the fatuity of the Grand Tour, ridiculed by the author in *The Fathers*[3] and elsewhere.

The paratactic form of *Joseph Andrews*, then, gives Fielding the opportunity to assemble a large number of the ideas previously disseminated in his works. He makes his novel still more didactically inclusive by the insertion of self-contained dialogues, dissertations, and even short essays. Fielding himself is quite explicit about his episodic manner. After expatiating at some length on High People and Low People, he continues: 'And now, reader, I hope thou wilt pardon this long digression, which seemed to me necessary to vindicate the great character of Mrs. Slipslop ... ' (book ii, ch. 13).[4] Another chapter begins:

Our travellers ... travelled many miles before they met with any adventure worth relating. In this interval we shall present our readers with a very curious discourse, as we apprehend it, concerning public schools, which passed between Mr. Joseph Andrews and Mr. Abraham Adams. (book iii, ch. 5)[5]

Some of the chapter-headings also suggest how far *Joseph Andrews* was constructed as a string of self-contained adventures, dialogues, and observations. One runs: 'A discourse between the poet and the player; of no other use in this history but to divert the reader' (book iii, ch. 10).[6] A chapter which comprises several such fragments can reflect

---

[1] Henley ed., i.234.   [2] Henley ed., xv.240 ff.
[3] In the character of Young Kennel.   [4] Henley ed., i.182.
[5] Henley ed., i.260.   [6] Henley ed., i.293.

the fact in the title: 'Sayings of wise men. A Dialogue between the lady and her maid; and a panegyric, or rather satire, on the passion of love, in the sublime style' (book i, ch. 7).[1]

The panegyric mentioned here is, of course, presented by Fielding himself, intervening as narrator. There are several such apostrophes and interludes in *Joseph Andrews*. Sometimes Fielding comments in a more particularized way, as in the description of Didapper (book iv, ch. 9),[2] or the attack on Scout:

> This Scout was one of those fellows who, without any knowledge of the law, or being bred to it, take upon them, in defiance of an act of Parliament, to act as lawyers in the country, and are called so. They are the pests of society, and a scandal to a profession to which indeed they do not belong, and which owes to such kind of rascallions the ill-will which weak persons bear towards it. (book iv, ch. 3)[3]

More generally, however, Fielding is able to propagate his own views through the conversations of his characters. Joseph holds forth on charity, Wilson on coquettes, patronage, and vanity, Adams on the duties of a clergyman, education, faith without works, and submission to the divine will. Often, also, comment is infiltrated into the novel by means of innuendo:

> '. . . it would do a man good to see his worship, our justice, commit a fellow to Bridewell, he takes so much pleasure in it; and when once we ha'un there, we seldom hear any more o'un. He's either starved or eat up by vermin in a month's time.' (book iv, ch. 3)[4]

The loose-leaf formula of *Joseph Andrews* thus gives Fielding, within the limits of Joseph's own story, the opportunity of making almost any point he wishes, either by embodying it in some directly enacted scene or by advancing it in a passage of direct or indirect didactic comment.

Demonstrating the pervasiveness of didacticism in *Joseph Andrews* entails a neglect of the book's most obvious and remarkable quality—its humour. The humorous and the didactic intention can co-exist because Fielding chooses to make most of his points through a satire as entertaining as

---

[1] Henley ed., i.43.   [2] Henley ed., i.355.
[3] Henley ed., i.324.   [4] Henley ed., i.323–4.

it is corrective. His province, he explains in the Preface, is 'the Ridiculous'; he specifically relegates 'great vices' to the background. In any case a number of incidents are included solely to amuse. But Fielding's primary intention in *Joseph Andrews*, as in his other novels, is without question didactic, and it is the didactic intention which determines the form and nature of the work.

2

The schematic approach which derives from Fielding's moral intention has an alienating effect. It constantly puts the narrative interest at the mercy of the didactic. A clear example of the subordination of story to satire is the account of the raid on the coach carrying the injured Joseph. Fielding describes it as casually as he has described the previous attack on Joseph himself: 'The lawyer was inquiring into the circumstances of the robbery, when the coach stopped, and one of the ruffians, putting a pistol in, demanded their money of the passengers, who readily gave it them . . . ' (book i, ch. 12).[1] When the passengers were deciding whether to help Joseph, an old gentleman cried 'let us make all the haste imaginable, or we shall be robbed too'. Yet in common with the other passengers he seems undisturbed by the robbery when it comes; in fact he makes no reference to it at all, but resumes chaffing Joseph. Since the incident has not the smallest narrative repercussions its only possible usefulness is that it further exposes the hypocrisy of the prude. She has just answered the lawyer's suggestion that she give Joseph a dram, by protesting that 'she never tasted any such thing'. But in the course of the robbery she hands over ' . . . a little silver bottle, of about a half-pint size, which the rogue, clapping it to his mouth, and drinking her health, declared held some of the best Nantes he had ever tasted . . . ' (book i, ch. 12).[2]

The incident is one of a number so lacking in plausible detail as to appear nothing more than means to a didactic end. The minor characters are in any case merely representatives of single moral attitudes. The cowardly braggart, for

[1] Henley ed., i.65.   [2] Henley ed., i.65.

example, or Miss Grave-airs, have no existence outside the one hypocritical impulse they embody. When the story seems to be most blatantly manipulated to highlight those impulses the novel takes on the air of a moral demonstration in which the characters serve only as models. The calmness with which Fielding proposes the imminent death of Joseph, or the imminent rape of Fanny, tends to reduce even his hero and heroine to this level of simple manœuvrability.

The truth to life of *Joseph Andrews* is also affected by Fielding's choice of narrative conventions; notably by the romantic tradition behind Joseph's story, and the picaresque tradition behind the account of the journey home. The portrayal of Joseph is initially influenced by the demands of parody: '. . . he retired into his own garret, and entered himself into an ejaculation on the numberless calamities which attended beauty, and the misfortune it was to be handsomer than one's neighbors' (book i, ch. 10).[1] Subsequently, however, he emerges simply as an amiable young man, protective towards Fanny, dutiful towards Parson Adams, and valiant in face of danger. As a model youth, first idealistically and then realistically, he tends to be a rather colourless figure, though this normality if anything serves to heighten the general plausibility of the characterization. Yet this worthily ordinary hero has to find fortune and his rightful parents by means of some highly implausible coincidences and discoveries. This is to say that the romantic plot belongs on a level of stylization different from that of much of the characterization in the book. The disparity is illustrated in the behaviour of Pamela's mother. After the pedlar has told his story: '. . . old Mrs. Andrews, running to Fanny, embraced her, crying out, "She is, she is my child!"' (book iv, ch. 15).[2] This is the formal romantic reaction. When the 'discoveries' are complete and the story is back on its normal course she is less emotional: 'Gammar Andrews kissed her, and said she was heartily glad to see her; but for her part, she could never love any one better than Joseph' (book iv, ch. 16).[3] Mrs. Andrews's snatch of rhetoric, and the events which occasion it, belong to a romantic convention which Fielding seems to invoke as the only means of

---

[1] Henley ed., i.56.   [2] Henley ed., i.384.   [3] Henley ed., i.388.

resolving his story. As in the plays, his formal method of organizing his material is discordantly artificial.

The story of the journey home, of course, tends to stylization in its sheer copiousness of incident. Far more important, however, is another result of picaresque influence—that the burlesque interludes, and notably the fights, seem overdrawn in relation to the rest of the action. Adams at different times is involved in four fights, getting soaked with urine in one of them and with hog's blood in a second. On other occasions he falls in the mire of a pig-sty, is attacked by a pack of hunting dogs, and finds himself in bed first with Slipslop and then with Fanny. Such incidents have a cheerful obviousness tolerable enough in itself, but clumsier than the usual manner of the incidents which help to characterize Adams.

These discrepancies of approach are worth labouring because they derive from Fielding's central problem of establishing a consistent narrative convention. His didactic scheme, and the formal pattern he constructed from the romance and the picaresque tale, could have combined to produce a consistently stylized moral fable. But he was also concerned to present a realistic picture of ordinary experience. The inadequate narrative realization of the robberies, the unlikelihood of Wilson's life consisting solely of a series of moral and financial crises, the abrupt and unexplained death of Sir Thomas Booby, all these seem inharmonious because they figure in a story where the narrative generally has a convincing life of its own. Not only are the adventures themselves credible enough (compare those of *Candide*, a moral fable proper) but the continuity between them is sustained by a great amount of trivial circumstantial detail which gives the novel an air of reality. For instance, Joseph, leaving the friend who has accompanied the first stage of his journey home, buys him a pint of wine, and thanks him for the favour of his horse (book i, ch. 12).[1] Fanny, when she hears of Joseph's injuries at the hands of the robbers:

... that instant abandoned the cow she was milking, and taking with her a little bundle of clothes under her arm, and all the money she was

---

[1] Henley ed., i.62.

worth in her own purse, without consulting any one, immediately set forward ... (book ii, ch. 10)[1]

When the three travellers leave the Wilsons:

The gentleman importuned them much to stay dinner; but when he found their eagerness to depart he summoned his wife; and accordingly, having performed all the usual ceremonies of bows and courtesies more pleasant to be seen than to be related, they took their leave, the gentleman and his wife heartily wishing them a good journey, and they as heartily thanking them for their kind entertainment. (book iii, ch. 5)[2]

Such passages are more than mere random gestures of verisimilitude. Because Fielding is preaching about the morality of everyday life it is essential for him to establish a context in which the standards of ordinary courtesy and humanity are seen to be important. The amicable farewells to Joseph's friend and to the Wilsons are in strong contrast to the parting words between the travellers and a grasping landlady:

... they all sailed out of the house without any compliments from their hostess, or indeed without paying her any, Adams declaring he would take particular care never to call there again, and she on her side assuring them she wanted no such guests. (book ii, ch. 15)[3]

Certainly realistic details of conduct and subsistence have an important narrative function: they help to prevent the story from resolving itself into a collection of fragments. They give some impression of a continuity of behaviour and relationships extending beyond what is revealed in the text alone. And passages of credible-sounding conversation assist the illusion:

'D—n me,' says the coachman, 'I will shoot with you, five guineas a shot.' 'You be hanged,' says the other; 'for five guineas you shall shoot at my a—.' 'Done,' says the coachman; 'I'll pepper you better than ever you was peppered by Jenny Bouncer.' 'Pepper your grandmother!' says the other: 'Here's Tow-wouse will let you shoot at him for a shilling a time.' (book i, ch. 16)[4]

It is true that this particular exchange has a partly satiric intention, but its total lack of relation to the story—neither

---

[1] Henley ed., i.167.   [2] Henley ed., i.259–60.
[3] Henley ed., i.196.   [4] Henley ed., i.88.

sportsman ever has anything to do with the travellers—and still more the sense of literal accuracy which the *non sequiturs* and the narrative irrelevance underline, make it seem like something overheard, and add to the sense of life going on around and outside the adventures recorded in the novel.

No doubt it was partly Fielding's adherence to the precept of Truth to Life which occasioned this realism of detail. But often the fidelity of idiom is carried over into dialogue clearly fulfilling a didactic function. As Cross points out, Fielding characteristically worked from observation to theory rather than the other way about.[1] He was not obliged to *invent* embodiments of the relevent abstract qualities; it was part of his purpose to use specific examples of such qualities which he had himself observed. Like Hogarth, he could work out a moral plan in terms of real-life instances. The first conversation between the Tow-wouses is a case in point:

'My dear,' said Mr. Tow-wouse, 'this is a poor wretch.' 'Yes,' says she, 'I know it is a poor wretch; but what the devil have we to do with poor wretches? The law makes us provide for too many already. We shall have thirty or forty poor wretches in red coats shortly.' 'My dear,' cries Tow-wouse, 'This man hath been robbed of all he hath.' 'Well, then,' said she, 'where's his money to pay his reckoning? Why doth not such a fellow go to an ale-house? I shall send him packing as soon as I am up, I assure you.' 'My dear,' said he, 'common charity won't suffer you to do that.' 'Common charity, a f—t!' says she ... (book i, ch. 12)[2]

The whole exchange is true to life in every expletive and inflection; and the importance of this realism of speech to Fielding's didactic purpose is considerable. He is presenting instances of meanness and hypocrisy particularly cogent because they reflect widespread and familiar attitudes. Mrs. Tow-wouse may incarnate a Hobbesian self-interest, but it is because she uses the phrases and cadences of a familiar style of selfishness that she is an effective didactic mechanism.

More than anything else, however, it is the completeness of the characterization of Parson Adams which gives the

---

[1] Cross, i.341.   [2] Henley ed., i.68.

novel an air of realism. There are two reasons for the exceptional fullness of this portrayal. One is that Fielding is clearly describing a character taken from his own circle of friends. Even in the author's lifetime Adams was identified with a certain Parson Young.[1] If Fielding's prefatory claim is accepted, that he drew nearly all the characters from his personal experience, then it is understandable that this portrayal should involve an intimacy of detail hardly present in the re-creation from memory of, say, an innkeeper or a coachman. Secondly Adams is clearly the embodiment of Fielding's positive precept of Good-nature, and as such has almost by definition to be drawn on a generous scale. The Goodnatured man, as was suggested in an earlier chapter, had not only to do good, but to feel an active sympathy with all the joys and sorrows of his fellow men. In other words a positive abundance of goodness and warmth was involved, which could only be suggested in a fictitious character by extrafunctional details of character and behaviour.

For both these reasons the character of Adams is developed to an extent larger than is essential to the part he plays in the action. Many of the oddities of his personality and conduct are of a kind to suggest, unverifiably, that Fielding is recalling real-life episodes. In any case they have the effect of exciting an interest in Adams for his own sake, of a kind which is not aroused by the other characters.

His absent-mindedness is depicted in a dozen extraneous incidents. The first time he is seen on his own he leaves an inn without remembering to pay for the board of his horse, wades through a stream up to his middle simply through failing to notice a nearby bridge, and finally has to ask a passerby the way to the nearest inn, although there is one clearly visible a stone's throw away.

In conversation he is made equally self-revealing. His active sympathy finds expression in a ready concern for the characters whose stories he hears: 'At these words Adams fetched a deep groan, which frighted the ladies, who told him "they hoped he was not ill." He answered, "He groaned only for the folly of Leonora"' (book ii, ch. 4).[2] When Wilson recounts the sad end of the girl he debauched,

[1] See Cross, i.344 ff.   [2] Henley ed., i.126.

he gives 'a deep sigh, which Mr. Adams echoed very loudly'. Adams is 'in a rapture' to hear of Harriet's generosity to Wilson, and he weeps with his host when the latter recalls the abduction of his first child.

Such reactions might be intended specifically as lively demonstrations of Good-natured warmth of feeling; but Adams's curiosity, which can have no particular moral significance, is made just as convincing. When there is a dispute as to whether the narrator of Leonora's history should repeat two letters written by the lovers, Adams contends for it 'with the utmost vehemence'. Later he interrupts the story to demand further information: '"Madam," said Adams, "if it be not impertinent, I should be glad to know how this gentleman was dressed"' (book ii, ch. 4).[1] Even details of Adams's appearance—his torn cassock, his large fist, and his long stride—have the authority of harmony and irrelevance. Of all the characters in the book he is the only one clearly developed for his own sake, and as such he affects the whole narrative balance.

There is one more important element in *Joseph Andrews* which disturbs the schematic plan, though in an entirely different way, and that is the characterization, or more particularly the motivation, of Lady Booby. With the very minor exception of Betty she is the only character who has to make a difficult choice of any kind. It seems fairly obvious, however, that the complexity of emotion she is endowed with is chiefly the product of narrative expediency; for it is the fluctuations of her attitude to Joseph which keep the plot in motion. She has to desire him, be angry enough at his rebuff to dismiss him and regretful enough to pursue him again. She must be sufficiently humiliated by his love for Fanny to take steps to have him condemned to Bridewell, and sufficiently infatuated to contemplate marriage with him when his love for Fanny seems doomed.

Fielding is obliged to suggest some sort of motive for all these changes of heart. By means of a number of soliloquies and descriptions he plausibly adjusts and readjusts the balance between pride and infatuation. Yet he also manages to develop such passages for their own sake. He makes Lady

[1] Henley ed., i.125.

Booby's emotional plight the occasion for a 'panegyric, or rather satire, on the passion of love, in the sublime style', and for a long reflection on female sexual psychology in general. At several points in the story his inserted didactic comments are concerned rather with human nature than with ethics. His account of Lady Booby's heart, even if forced on him by the plot, may well have shown him some of the possibilities of a closer study of feeling than the general plan of his novel permitted him.

3

There was little in *Joseph Andrews* that was essentially original. Its moral attitudes are those which underlie all Fielding's serious writing, and many even of the specific points had been made in previous works. Fielding had also written an earlier parody of *Pamela* which, if ribald, aimed at a serious exposure of the book's implicit hypocrisy; and as early as 1728, when he began *Don Quixote in England*, he had used the Cervantesque formula to satirize certain aspects of English society.

In *Joseph Andrews* Fielding was employing all these elements, together with some character-sketches and dialogues drawn from personal observation, as the ingredients of a new form, the comi-prosai-epic. The chief interest of the finished book from the point of view of literary history is the fact that its author has somehow found a means of fusing his diverse materials into a coherent whole. He has done so, moreover, despite the fact that both his moral intention and his narrative intention are inherently contradictory. From a didactic point of view Fielding required an artificial convention of plot and character, which would enable him to shape the episodes into a series of parables. Yet the general tenor had to be realistic, in order to lend point to the very practical terms of the moralizing. From the narrative point of view the only available formal discipline was the artificial romantic plot; yet much of Fielding's material was taken direct from real life.

As might be expected, this ambivalence of intention gives the novel a somewhat spasmodic quality. The aspects of reality on which the author chooses to place emphasis are not consistently chosen. For instance, during the journey home, when the poverty of the travellers is the cause of most of their adventures, Fielding records their financial state in detail. When they reach their destination, however, the interest is centred on Lady Booby's machinations, and there is no explanation of how Joseph and Fanny, both of whom are destitute, find food and shelter. Again, certain minor characters are described in detail—Didapper, for example, and Mrs. Tow-wouse—but there is no direct description of Lady Booby, or, oddly enough, of Parson Adams. Above all, as the second part of this chapter tried to show, the narrative shifts between several levels of verisimilitude.

Yet critics have rarely spoken of this very experimental novel as being anything short of a balanced, articulated whole, and it is not difficult to see why. In the first place almost everything that happens in the book is ultimately plausible. All the main adventures occur in the course of a single English journey, and none of the characters is outside the range of ordinary experience.

Also important is the novel's prevailing lightness of tone. Fielding's ironic, alienating style of narration muffles any potential seriousness in the incidents. The robberies, the attempted rapes, the threatened imprisonments, are never felt as real dangers. As Fielding claims in the Preface, those 'great vices' which do figure in the novel 'never produce the intended evil'. Consequently such characters as Lady Booby or the 'roasting' squire never seem as vicious as their actions ought to make them seem, and are rather ridiculed than condemned. On the other hand, of the book's two heroes Parson Adams is a comic, and Joseph a mock-heroic, figure; without belittling them Fielding need never take either completely seriously. Even the graver dialogues and the moralizing are usually comic in tone.

What has happened is that Fielding has instinctively played down those elements which threaten to take him outside the province of everyday comic incident and everyday morality. The novel has consequently a coherence in matter and manner which has led to its being taken for granted as an assured totality. But this coherence is something less than Fielding was aiming at. The range of his material is wider than the effective range of his finished novel. The broader of the burlesque scenes, the description of Didapper, the squalid realities of Wilson's youthful career, Adams's dignified defiance of Lady Booby's threats—none of these features is subsumed under the general convention of *Joseph Andrews*. Even the moral intention of the book is partly gelded by its manner, as is shown by the way in which critics have consistently stressed other virtues in the novel: its variety, its characterization, its humour.

Fielding therefore constructs a narrative presenting a fairly consistent picture of life at the expense of writing a rather smaller novel than he intended. None the less he had shown that the prose narrative could embody moral ideas and be subjected to formal discipline. He had experimented with different ways of projecting character and motive, different ways of infiltrating didactic comment and different ways of drawing on real-life experience. It was open to him in his next novel to use the knowledge he had gained about his new form to construct a larger-scale narrative, embodying a more comprehensive set of moral views.

VII

TOM JONES

R.s. CRANE suggests in an article that the 'unifying idea' which holds *Tom Jones* together is:

> ... the dynamic system of actions, extending throughout the novel, by which the divergent intentions and beliefs of a large number of persons ... are made to co-operate, with the assistance of Fortune, first to bring Tom into an incomplete and precarious union ... with Allworthy and Sophia; then to separate him as completely as possible from them through actions that impel both of them, one after the other, to reverse their opinions of his character; and then, just as he seems about to fulfil the old prophecy that 'he was certainly born to be hanged,' to restore them unexpectedly to him in a more entire and stable union of both affection and fortune than he has known before.[1]

This is an adequate statement of what happens in the story, but it overlooks the moral significance which makes the novel more than a romance with an artificial plot. Fielding states, in his dedication to *Tom Jones*, that 'to recommend goodness and innocence hath been my sincere endeavour in this history'.[2] Although the claim seems conventional it is markedly different from the intentions outlined in the Preface to *Joseph Andrews*. In that book Fielding's concern is with 'the true Ridiculous', of which 'the only source' is affectation.[3] His aim is primarily the negative one of exposing various vices and follies. Parson Adams, the exemplar of his positive precept of Good-nature, is therefore largely a passive figure, serving as a touchstone for the worth of the people with whom he is brought into contact. In *Tom Jones*, although it is again part of Fielding's intention 'to laugh mankind out of their favourite follies and vices',[4]

---

[1] 'The Plot of *Tom Jones*', *Journal of General Education*, iv (1950), 112 ff.

[2] Henley ed., iii.12. [3] Henley ed., i.21.

[4] Dedication; Henley ed., iii.12–13.

the emphasis is clearly to be rather the positive one of promoting virtue.

The same basic antithesis of charity and self-interest is expounded, however. Tom's youthful generosities to Black George's family are designed to show him as essentially the Good-natured Man. In any case the author is quite explicit about the humanity of his hero:

... he was one who could truly say with him in Terence, *Homo sum: humani nihil a me alienum puto.* He was never an indifferent spectator of the misery or happiness of any one; and he felt either the one or the other in great proportion as he himself contributed to either. (book xv, ch. 8)[1]

This is exactly the kind of warm concern for others which Fielding implies in his several definitions of Good-nature, and which is embodied in Parson Adams. As was suggested in the preceding chapter, however, Adams only shares the role of hero in *Joseph Andrews.* Joseph, in other respects a rather colourless figure, is the narrative centre of the book, the fulfilling of his romantic aspirations constituting the plot. Parson Adams is the didactic centre, round whom Fielding is able to develop the series of moral episodes which compose the substance of the novel. To a great extent Tom combines these two roles. Clearly he is the romantic hero of the story, but he is also, as will be shown, the focus of didactic interest.

The negative side of the antithesis, the representation of hypocrisy, is similarly more crystallized than in *Joseph Andrews.* A variety of false values are epitomized by the single person of Blifil. The chief difference between the didactic content of the two novels, however, does not lie in the greater refinement that this more complex personification suggests, but in the fact that Fielding is less interested in displaying the falsity of Blifil than in showing the strengths and weaknesses of Tom. In the dedication he declares his intention of proving that virtue brings more rewards than vice:

For this purpose I have shown that no acquisitions of guilt can compensate the loss of that solid inward comfort of mind, which is the sure

[1] Henley ed., v.178.

companion of innocence and virtue; nor can in the least balance the evil of that horror and anxiety which, in their room, guilt introduces into our bosoms. And again, that as these acquisitions are in themselves generally worthless, so are the means to attain them not only base and infamous, but at best incertain, and always full of danger. Lastly, I have endeavoured strongly to inculcate, that virtue and innocence can scarce ever be injured but by indiscretion; and that it is this alone which often betrays them into the snares that deceit and villainy spread for them.[1]

These are stock themes of Fielding's which found little expression in *Joseph Andrews*. It is notable that they are all illustrated by the reactions of Tom rather than those of Blifil. Despite his constant deceit it is only when unmasked that Blifil shows 'horror and anxiety', and he never seems to feel that the objects of his machinations are 'worthless'. It is Tom who is overcome by remorse at his comparatively minor sins, and appalled at their consequences. And above all it is Tom whose 'indiscretions' betray him into the traps spread by Blifil's 'deceit and villainy'. This point is underlined by Fielding in Book III, chapter 7, 'In which the author himself makes his appearance on the stage.' In this very deliberate intervention he announces that Tom's adventures will:

. . . if rightly understood, afford a very useful lesson to those well-disposed youths who shall hereafter be our readers; for they may here find that goodness of heart and openness of temper . . . will by no means, alas! do their business in the world. Prudence and circumspection are necessary even to the best of men . . . no man can be good enough to enable him to neglect the rules of prudence; nor will Virtue herself look beautiful unless she be bedecked with the outward ornaments of decency and decorum. And this precept, my worthy disciples, if you read with due attention, you will, I hope, find sufficiently enforced by examples in the following pages.[2]

The point is emphasized again at other crucial moments in the narrative. Allworthy, on what he thinks to be his death-bed, puts it to Tom himself: '"I am convinced, my child, that you have much goodness, generosity, and honor in your temper; if you will add prudence and religion to these, you must be happy . . . "' (book v, ch. 7).[3] When

---

[1] Henley ed., iii.12.   [2] Henley ed., iii.131–2.   [3] Henley ed., iii.243.

reconciled with Tom at the end of the novel he recalls this counsel:

'You now see, Tom, to what dangers imprudence alone may subject virtue ... Prudence is indeed the duty which we owe to ourselves; and if we will be so much our own enemies as to neglect it, we are not to wonder if the world is deficient in discharging their duty to us ... ' (book xviii, ch. 10)[1]

It is indiscretion which has by then betrayed Tom into a knowledge of the miseries which the guilty man must suffer. As the next section will show, the misfortunes Crane mentions befall Tom as the result of various imprudent deeds, and his ultimate return to favour is the reward of his true good-nature. Fielding is 'promoting the cause of virtue' by showing some of the pitfalls it must avoid: 'A moral which I have the more industriously laboured, as the teaching it is, of all others, the likeliest to be attended with success; since, I believe, it is much easier to make good men wise, than to make bad men good' (Dedication).[2]

This is an idea demanding a much more intricate narrative embodiment than that of *Joseph Andrews*, a movement away from the fairly simple personification of the moral fable. The central character must be more complex, must be allowed to do wrong, and eventually—since the book, as a comedy, is to end happily—must be shown as developing a new discretion. Moreover since the hero's active goodness, and more particularly his imprudence, can only be demonstrated through positive deeds and their repercussions, he must be shown to be much more in control of, and responsible for, his own destiny. Altogether, in fact, the didactic plan of *Tom Jones* demands a narrative projection a good deal closer to the modern novel, in its complexity, than *Joseph Andrews* was.

At the same time, however, the narrative plan seems to have become more ambitious in its own right. It is true that there are certain general similarities to *Joseph Andrews*—the plot is founded on a mystery of birth, and deals in thwarted love eventually fulfilled. Like the earlier novel, *Tom Jones* is divided into a period passed in London, a journey, and a

[1] Henley ed., v.346.　　[2] Henley ed., iii.12.

period passed in the country, though here the order is reversed.

In *Tom Jones*, however, the plot is much more elaborate and ingenious. The final 'discovery' of Tom's parentage is brought about by a series of events to which almost every incident in the book has directly or indirectly contributed. Fielding himself several times draws attention to the relevance of even the most minor happenings. In short, this plot is far more artificial, and therefore more constricting, than that of *Joseph Andrews*.

In general structure, too, the novel is more sophisticated. It is divided into eighteen books, of which six are concerned with the country, six with the journey, and six with the town. Each book is prefaced with an introductory chapter. Not only unity of action is observed but, from the moment of Tom's banishment, unity of time, an exact scheme of dates and hours being pursued, in which even the phases of the moon tally with the almanac.[1]

Incidental entertainment in the picaresque tradition, by means of fights, mock-heroics, and comic dialogues, remains part of the intention. But *Tom Jones* is very clearly designed as a complex artifact of which almost every detail is calculated and relevant. Fielding's literary programme is thus as demanding as his didactic one, and it is not surprising that the two are sometimes impossible to reconcile.

I

Because the plot of *Tom Jones*, unlike that of *Joseph Andrews*, involves a 'system of actions', the moral argument is less close to the surface than that of its predecessor. Tom's good deeds and indiscretions do not usually bring immediate reward or retribution, but rather initiate sequences of action which prove in the long run to be advantageous or disadvantageous. Moreover they only produce these effects because of the elaborate context of Tom's unknown parentage, and adoption into a largely hostile household. In tracing the main didactic theme of the book, therefore, it is necessary to disregard much of the narrative

[1] See Cross, ii.188 ff.

which merely establishes or develops various features of the plot. Fielding has to devote several chapters even of *Joseph Andrews*, with its relatively simple story, to the foundation of his plot. In *Tom Jones* both the first two books are needed to bring the story up to date.

Even Books III and IV are largely expository; but it is to be noted that Fielding makes them serve a double purpose. Not only is the contrast between Tom and Blifil established, but four major characters are introduced—Western, Sophia, Thwackum, and Square—and the first hint is given of the impending romance between Tom and Sophia. The whole section suggests an advance in technique in that, unlike most of *Joseph Andrews*, it contributes both to the action and to the moral purpose.

The story proper displays a similar inter-involvement of action and theme, its chief didactic point being made through the plot. Perhaps the most emphatic evidence that the fluctuations of fortune described by Crane are expressly conceived as punishments and rewards for Tom's imprudence and his good-nature, is supplied by Tom's own very explicit attitude during adversity. When visited in prison by Mrs. Waters he

... lamented the follies and vices of which he had been guilty; every one of which, he said, had been attended with such ill consequences that he should be unpardonable if he did not take warning, and quit those vicious courses for the future. (book xvii, ch. 9)[1]

The nadir of Tom's ill-luck is Partridge's disclosure that Mrs. Waters, whom he slept with at Upton, is his own mother. After his first despair Tom again faces the fact that it is his own conduct which has brought disaster: 'I am myself the cause of all my misery. All the dreadful mischiefs which have befallen me are the consequences only of my own folly and vice' (book xviii, ch. 2).[2] When eventually extricated from his various predicaments and reunited with Allworthy, Tom tells him:

'... believe me, my dear uncle, my punishment hath not been thrown away upon me: though I have been a great, I am not a hardened sinner; I thank Heaven, I have had time to reflect on my past life,

[1] Henley ed., v.291.   [2] Henley ed., v.296.

where, though I cannot charge myself with any gross villainy, yet I can discern follies and vices more than enough to repent and to be ashamed of; follies which have been attended with dreadful consequences to myself, and have brought me to the brink of destruction.' (book xviii, ch. 10)[1]

Clearly the reader is meant to see Tom's story, as he himself so specifically does, as a series of follies bringing eventual retribution. Though Tom's misfortunes are not simply the direct consequences of wrong-doing, as for example was Wilson's venereal disease, they do ultimately derive from it. He commits four major indiscretions, and in each case a chain of unlucky circumstances brings about a painful result.

His affair with Molly Seagrim comes to light purely by chance. Sophia, hearing of the Seagrims' plight from Tom, sends them some money and clothes. The vain Molly wears some of the finery to church, thereby so exciting the jealousy of her acquaintances that a fight ensues in the churchyard. A travelling fiddler, injured in the brawl, applies to All-worthy for a warrant, and in the course of the subsequent inquiry Molly's pregnancy is disclosed. The outcome of the affair is not very damaging to Tom. Although Sophia resolves to stifle what she now realizes to be her love for him, circumstances soon cause her to change her mind. The worst of the repercussions is that Square is able to suggest that Tom's previous kindnesses to the Seagrims have been motivated by lust for Molly, an insinuation which 'stamped on the mind of Allworthy the first bad impression concerning Jones'.[2]

Tom's second indiscretion is his misconduct during All-worthy's illness. Meeting Molly by chance, he is making love with her when surprised by Thwackum and Blifil, and he fights them both off rather than expose the identity of his mistress. The consequences are in this case grave enough. Tom is turned away by Allworthy, thereby being 'separated as completely as possible' from his guardian. Yet these results only ensue through the malice of Blifil, who mis-represents the whole matter, and the ill-luck of the affair's

---

[1] Henley ed., v.346.   [2] Book iv, ch. 2; Henley ed., iii.190.

being revealed at a time when Tom is too upset over Sophia to defend himself properly.

Though it is Tom's expulsion from Allworthy's household which physically separates him from Sophia, she herself does not 'reverse her opinion of his character' until learning of his behaviour with Mrs. Waters. Thereupon she leaves Upton without seeing him, convinced that '"he is not only a villain, but a low despicable wretch"'.[1] (book x, ch. 5)

To punish this instance of Tom's folly Fielding has to contrive not only that Sophia shall leave home, but that she shall arrive at the same inn as her lover just after he has succumbed to Mrs. Waters. He has also to arrange that her father shall reach the same hostelry next morning, since it is his intervention which prevents Tom making an immediate pursuit of Sophia. The morally remedial outcome of Tom's weakness—that he comes later to believe he has committed incest—depends on the large coincidence of his having chanced to rescue the same Jenny Jones who had admitted to being his mother.

Tom's final error, his liaison with Lady Bellaston, depends less on contrivance of plot to produce its unpleasant results. He naturally meets her in the course of seeing Sophia, and it is not unnatural that jealousy should cause her to initiate a plan to punish her lover and her rival. But even here coincidence plays some part in the punishment of Tom. The press-gang sent to capture him happens to arrive at the very moment of his victorious duel with Fitzpatrick, and it is only through the agency of these men that he is arrested and accused of starting the fight.

Fielding makes some effort to place these misdemeanours in an appropriate light, stressing that Tom falls through folly rather than vice. It is emphasized that each of the women takes an active part in seducing him, that he thinks himself in love with Molly in the first instance, and that all his subsequent lapses occur when he seems to have no hope of gaining Sophia. None the less Tom is justified in seeing his final accumulation of misfortunes as the consequence of his previous errors. He has been turned away by Allworthy and finally abandoned by Sophia, as a result of his affairs with

[1] Henley ed., iv.217.

Molly and with Lady Bellaston; he is imprisoned and apparently guilty of incest as a result of his affair with Mrs. Waters. That his plight should be so appropriately punitive, and bear out so clearly the moral that Fielding states in his dedication and recalls at regular intervals in the narrative, makes it plain that the plot has been designed and manipulated specifically to a didactic end. That is to say that the whole structure of the novel, like that of *Joseph Andrews*, is subordinated to the moral intention.

Tom's eventual good fortune is less explicitly a reward for his good deeds. His return to favour depends chiefly on the realization by Allworthy and Sophia of his true merit. Nevertheless certain of his worthy actions have repercussions which help to effect his ultimate prosperity. Mrs. Waters, whom he rescues from imminent murder, pays tribute to his character before Allworthy, and happens to be able to solve the mystery of Tom's parentage. Mrs. Miller, who reveres Tom not only for promoting her daughter's marriage with Nightingale but also for preserving her cousin Anderson and his family, staunchly supports him before both Allworthy and Sophia, to each of whom she tells the full story of her obligations. It is through her agency, too, that Sophia comes to hear of another of Tom's commendable actions, his refusal of an advantageous match with Mrs. Hunt:

' . . . when I mentioned the young lady's name, who is no other than the pretty widow Hunt, I thought she turned pale; but when I said you had refused her, I will be sworn her face was all over scarlet in an instant; and these were her very words: I will not deny but that I believe he has some affection for me.' (book xviii, ch. 10)[1]

The incident of Mrs. Hunt relates to another tendency in some of Tom's 'good' actions: they justify his claim to Allworthy and Sophia that he has learned wisdom from his past errors. Not only does he reject the rich widow's tempting offer, he also resists the blandishments of Mrs. Fitzpatrick: ' . . . for, faulty as he hath hitherto appeared in this history, his whole thoughts were now so confined to his Sophia that I believe no woman upon earth could have now drawn him into an act of inconstancy' (book xvi, ch. 9).[2]

---

[1] Henley ed., v.350.   [2] Henley ed., v.242.

This new maturity in Tom suggests that he will now be able to foster the good fortune he has long deserved.

The plot of *Tom Jones*, it has been suggested, is designed to bring home to the hero himself, and to the reader, the dangers of imprudence. But since it is only through elaborate processes of coincidence and intrigue that retribution is made to descend, the simple moral intention is rather submerged in the complex execution. If the novel none the less shows a strong ethical concern it is because Fielding contrives to insert a great deal of local didactic comment in his usual vein.

He can do this the more easily in that *Tom Jones*, although its main theme is worked out rather in terms of character than of incident, quickly resolves into the episodic manner. When Fielding is first delineating the characters of Tom and Blifil, he resorts to a technique of direct illustration after only three paragraphs: 'An incident which happened about this time will set the characters of these two lads more fairly before the discerning reader than is in the power of the longest dissertation' (book iii, ch. 2).[1] The anecdote in question extends over five chapters. Two further chapters in the same book also contain complete episodes: 'A childish incident, in which, however, is seen a good-natured disposition in Tom Jones' (book iii, ch. 8),[2] and 'Containing an incident of a more heinous kind, with the comments of Thwackum and Square' (book iii, ch. 9).[3] After introducing Sophia at the beginning of Book IV, Fielding relates another such event: 'Wherein the history goes back to commemorate a trifling incident that happened some years since; but which, trifling as it was, had some future consequences' (book iii, ch. 3).[4]

These episodes are, of course, chiefly designed to illustrate the difference in character between Tom and Blifil, but subsidiary didactic points are also made. The pattern in this section of the novel is for incident to be succeeded by discussion, and Fielding makes the chief disputants hold views which he proceeds to satirize. Square is a deist and Thwackum virtually a Methodist; Fielding exposes what he regards as the absurdity of their beliefs by contrasting their

[1] Henley ed., iii.108.   [2] Henley ed., iii.132.
[3] Henley ed., iii.135.   [4] Henley ed., iii.149.

learned, but partial and wrong-headed, reactions to Tom's escapades, with the common-sense views of Allworthy, and even of Bridget, and Squire Western.[1]

Both Thwackum and Square have a part to play in the narrative—a part to which the ethical beliefs Fielding imposes on them are quite irrelevant. Characters and incidents all through *Tom Jones*, although marshalled to serve the purposes of the complex plot, are frequently used in this way to make minor didactic points. For instance when Allworthy shows the infant he has just discovered in his bed, to his maidservant, Mrs. Wilkins, she at once exclaims against it:

> 'Faugh! how it stinks! It doth not smell like a Christian. If I might be so bold to give my advice, I would have it put in a basket, and sent out and laid at the churchwarden's door. It is a good night, only a little rainy and windy . . . ' (book i, ch. 3)[2]

When both her master and mistress speak in Tom's favour she quickly changes her tune: ' . . . she fell to squeezing and kissing . . . crying out, in a shrill voice, "O, the dear little creature!—The dear, sweet, pretty creature! Well, I vow it is as fine a boy as ever was seen!"' (book i, ch. 5).[3]

The only essential narrative issue at this juncture is the introduction of Tom to the Allworthy household. Fielding enlarges on the essentials to make the kind of satirical point he makes against Mrs. Tow-wouse in *Joseph Andrews*. Similarly, although it is for a narrative purpose that Tom has to break his arm—it is because he injures himself in saving her, that Sophia begins to fall in love with him—Fielding again makes didactic capital of the situation. Square is lecturing Tom on the contemptibility of physical suffering, when he bites his tongue, and breaks into muttered oaths of pain.[4] It is the same kind of 'reversal' by which in *Joseph Andrews* Fielding shows the discrepancy between philosophical theory and practice.[5] His former didactic method is still functioning alongside the new.

---

[1] (e.g.) Book iii, chs. 3, 8, 9; book iv, ch. 4; Henley ed., iii.121, 134, 136, 155.

[2] Henley ed., iii.25.   [3] Henley ed., iii.30.

[4] Book v, ch. 2; Henley ed., iii.212.

[5] Book iv, ch. 8; Henley ed., i.349 ff.

Since the incidents in *Tom Jones* have almost always to produce some particular result necessary to the plot, they can rarely be as autonomously didactic as the loosely strung adventures of *Joseph Andrews*. But when Tom and Sophia are travelling to London the narrative demands only that they take certain routes and meet certain people, so that Fielding has reasonable scope to make his episodes fulfil a second function. Tom's encounter with the Gypsies develops into an oblique comment on the law of criminal conversation;[1] the affair of the puppet-show is a jibe at the morality of the contemporary stage.[2] It is in this section of the novel, too, that both the long interpolated stories appear. Not only do these furnish, in Crane's term, 'negative analogies' to the situation of Tom and Sophia, they constitute attacks on misanthropy—one of Fielding's recurrent targets—and the kind of repressive marriage he had already exposed in *The Champion*.[3]

The characters encountered on the journey are also put to didactic use. The worthy lieutenant who befriends Tom has gained no promotion for nearly forty years, because his wife—whose charms have presumably weathered well— refuses to sleep with his commanding officer.[4] Yet again Fielding points to the corruptness of current practice in military preferment. The surgeon who attends Tom after he has been injured by Northerton, is another of Fielding's magniloquent quacks: '" ... the aliment will not be concreted, nor assimilated into chyle, and so will corrode the vascular orifices, and thus will aggravate the febrific symptoms"' (book viii, ch. 3).[5]

The chapters on London contain a greater proportion of sheer plot, but even here Fielding finds opportunity to be didactic. He makes his characteristic attacks on the manners and morals of high society, and ridicules various fashionable diversions, such as drums and masquerades.[6]

[1] Book xii, ch. 12; Henley ed., v.17–18.
[2] Book xii, chs. 5–6; Henley ed., iv.321–5.
[3] Henley ed., xv.185 ff. The story told there has some close affinities with Mrs. Fitzpatrick's.
[4] Book vii, ch. 12; Henley ed., iv.31.
[5] Henley ed., iv.72.
[6] (e.g.) Book xiii, ch. 7; book xvii, ch. 6; Henley ed., v.65; 274.

These examples should be sufficient to show how Fielding manipulates the incidents and characters involved in the plot of *Tom Jones* so that they embody, as do those in *Joseph Andrews*, a series of specific ethical ideas. He also makes use of the other didactic methods of his earlier novel. Once again he moralizes both *in propria persona* and through the mouths of his characters. The chapter-headings: 'Containing a few common matters, with a very uncommon observation upon them' (book i, ch. 5),[1] and 'Consisting partly of facts, and partly of observations upon them' (book xv, ch. 10)[2] suggest, as is in fact the case, that Fielding frequently slows down the narrative in order to comment directly or indirectly on some happening in the story. His tale naturally provides him with frequent texts for homilies on Good-nature, indiscretion, the cruelty of arranged marriages, or the joys of benevolence; but he finds many other incentives to moralizing in the course of the narration. There is 'a short apology for those people who overlook imperfections in their friends'[3] for instance, and 'a short digression in favor of the female sex'.[4] Such reflections are acknowledged in the chapter-title only when, like these, they develop considerable length, but they occur everywhere in the book. As early as his second chapter Fielding claims leave to digress as often as he thinks fit, and the digressions are usually didactic. It is to be noticed, however, that many of them are merely comments on human nature:

. . . though envy is at best a very malignant passion, yet is its bitterness greatly heightened by mixing with contempt towards the same object; and very much afraid I am, that whenever an obligation is joined to these two, indignation and not gratitude will be the product of all three. (book i, ch. 13)[5]

By making Allworthy a virtually perfect character, Fielding has provided himself with a ready-made didactic mouthpiece, and he takes full advantage of him. Allworthy reads Jenny a full-scale sermon on chastity, and Dr. Blifil a lecture

---

[1] Henley ed., iii.30.   [2] Henley ed., v.186.
[3] Book ii, ch. 7; Henley ed., iii.92.
[4] Book iv, ch. 13; Henley ed., iii.194.   [5] Henley ed., iii.63.

on the foundation of a happy marriage. He engages with
Captain Blifil on the meaning of Charity, and expatiates on
Death when on his sick-bed. Tom himself is permitted a
share of the moralizing. He states Fielding's own condemnation of the sort of misanthropy expressed by the Man of the
Hill; and he is even made to lecture Nightingale on sexual
morality. Sophia and Mrs. Miller are others who deliver
moral discourses on a variety of topics.

Throughout the novel Fielding is didactic in a more
general 'epic' way, introducing all kinds of information and
anecdotes from both modern and classical sources: the story
of Nell Gwynn's footman,[1] for example, or of the drunken
Cleostratus.[2] And apart from his direct moralizing he
insinuates his opinions on certain subjects in a variety of
minor ways, ranging from comparison: ' ... it is certain
they were no more in the right road to Coventry than the
fraudulent, griping, cruel, canting miser is in the right
road to heaven' (book xii, ch. 11),[3] to the use of footnotes:

> This is the second person of low condition whom we have recorded
> in this history to have sprung from the clergy. It is to be hoped such
> instances will, in future ages, when some provision is made for the
> families of the inferior clergy, appear stranger than they can be
> thought at present. (book iv, ch. 14)[4]

Many of the interludes in *Tom Jones*, however, are still
intended solely to entertain. Where the plot is at its thinnest,
for example during the journey of Sophia, whole chapters
can consist of little but brief narrative items, comic dialogues,
and snippets of comment. Again chapter-titles can reveal
this miscellaneous quality:

> The morning introduced in some pretty writing. A stage-coach.
> The civility of chamber-maids. The heroic temper of Sophia. Her
> generosity. The return to it. The departure of the company, and their
> arrival at London; with some remarks for the use of travellers
> (book xi, ch. 9)[5]

---

[1] Book xi, ch. 8; Henley ed., iv.285.
[2] Book v, ch. 10; Henley ed., iii.258.
[3] Henley ed., iv.348.   [4] Henley ed., iii.201.   [5] Henley ed., iv.290.

for instance, or: 'Containing little more than a few old observations' (book xii, ch. 9).[1]

These various practices combine to prevent *Tom Jones*
from becoming in fact what in theory it could have been:
a novel whose moral significance was expressed wholly
through its characters and the complex plot in which they are
involved. Despite its more sophisticated didactic plan it still
retains some of the loose-leaf, episodic quality of *Joseph
Andrews*.

2

Both Fielding's didactic scheme and the plot in which he
embodies it require that Tom should be more strongly
individualized than was Joseph Andrews. His character as
a good-natured but imprudent young man is essential to the
action. Two other figures in the novel, Allworthy and
Sophia, are based on people whom Fielding greatly revered:
his patron, Ralph Allen,[2] and his first wife, Charlotte.[3]
They too, therefore, are taken seriously. Fielding does not,
as in *Joseph Andrews*, merely subject his leading characters
to a succession of accidents, but to a great extent founds his
plot on the personalities of the three protagonists.

The result is that *Tom Jones* is a much more realistic novel
than *Joseph Andrews* in the sense of conveying the existential
quality of people and places. Fielding buttresses this sense of
reality by observing certain formal standards of verisimilitude. His hero and heroine grow up on neighbouring estates
in a fairly exact Somersetshire location. Their separate
journeys are described with scrupulous concern for time and
geography, and their final adventures take place in a series
of precisely specified locales in London.[4] Moreover real-life
characters such as Mrs. Whitefield[5] and Beau Nash[6] make
brief appearances, and the final two-thirds of the book is

---

[1] Henley ed., iv.338.

[2] See Cross, ii.162 ff.

[3] Book iv, ch. 2; book xiii, ch. 1; Henley ed., iii.146–7; v.31.

[4] (e.g.) Tom is imprisoned in the Gatehouse, Mrs. Miller's home is in
Bond Street, and Squire Western's lodgings are in Piccadilly.

[5] Book viii, ch. 8; Henley ed., iv.92 ff.

[6] Book xi, ch. 4; Henley ed., iv, 262–3.

set against the background of the '45. Perhaps this last point is as significant as any in revealing Fielding's intentions; the invasion has very little bearing on the plot, and can therefore serve only to lend circumstantiality to the events of the narrative.

Fielding is also much freer with realistic details of travelling, eating, and drinking than in *Joseph Andrews*. When recovering from the injury he received from Northerton: 'Jones swallowed a large mess of chicken, or rather cock, broth, with a very good appetite, as indeed he would have done the cock it was made of, with a pound of bacon into the bargain . . .' (book vii, ch. 14).[1] As in the previous novel, gratuitous passages of naturalistic dialogue contribute to the sense of actuality:

'The road to Bristol!' cries the fellow, scratching his head: 'Why, measter, I believe you will hardly get to Bristol this way tonight.' 'Prithee friend, then,' answered Jones, 'do tell us which is the way.' 'Why, measter,' cries the fellow, 'you must be come out of your road the Lord knows whither; for thick way goeth to Glocester.' 'Well, and which way goes to Bristol?' said Jones. 'Why, you be going away from Bristol,' answered the fellow. (book vii, ch. 10)[2]

Fielding is interestingly explicit on one occasion about this use of realistic detail. He has described how Mrs. Miller's little girl wept to hear of the imprisonment of Jones, 'who used to call her his little wife, and not only gave her many playthings, but spent whole hours in playing with her himself'. The author goes on:

Some readers may, perhaps, be pleased with these minute circumstances, in relating of which we follow the example of Plutarch, one of the best of our brother historians; and others, to whom they may appear trivial, will, we hope, at least pardon them, as we are never prolix on such occasions. (book xvii, ch. 2)[3]

Fielding consistently styles himself a 'historian', of course, but unlike the true historian he has to fabricate his own reality. The more frequent introduction of such 'minute circumstances' as those mentioned in the passages quoted above implies that in *Tom Jones* this 'reality' will be closer to everyday experience than it was in *Joseph Andrews*.

[1] Henley ed., iv.46.　　[2] Henley ed., iv.20–21.　　[3] Henley ed., v.253.

That the episodes composing the plot are to some extent
modified by this changed emphasis, can be seen by an examination of particular incidents: Tom's last adventure before
reaching London is a convenient example.[1] He is riding
towards Highgate with Partridge and a guide, when 'a
genteel-looking man, but upon a very shabby horse' asks if
he may join them. The four proceed for some time, making
conversation, till the stranger pulls out a pistol and demands
from Tom the one-hundred-pound note he knows him to be
carrying. Tom, though proferring all his own money,
refuses to surrender the note, and when the highwayman
threatens to shoot, he seizes the pistol and soon overpowers
him. His assailant begs for mercy, claiming that this is his
first robbery and that he has been driven to it by the distress
'of five hungry children, and a wife lying in of the sixth'.
After testing the truth of his story Tom releases him and
gives him a couple of guineas. The man returns home
promising never to resort to crime again.

Unlike the two highway robberies in *Joseph Andrews*, this
one has a part to play in the total story. Tom's readiness to
help even the man who has tried to steal from him is one of
the most striking demonstrations of his good-nature.
Furthermore the highwayman, unlike those of the earlier
novel, is to reappear. It later transpires that he is a cousin of
Tom's landlady, Mrs. Miller, and it is gratitude for this
kindness to her relative that prompts her bold and effective championing of Tom before Allworthy and Sophia. So
this encounter, as well as illustrating Tom's basic goodness,
is instrumental in rewarding it, and therefore relevant to
both theme and plot.

The actuality of *Tom Jones* as a whole is enhanced by the
continuity of detail from episode to episode. Here there is a
sound motive for the robbery in the hundred-pound note of
Sophia's which Tom has found. Quite plausibly his possession of it is made known through the chatter of Partridge,
who has been characterized throughout by thoughtless
garrulity. The courage and activity which enable Tom to
overpower his attacker have also been previously displayed in

---

[1] Book xii, ch. 14; Henley ed., v.26 ff.

the novel. These are hardly significant, being merely by-products of his status as a hero; but the sword with which he stands guard over his opponent is a notable detail in the book's continuity. Tom buys it to fight a duel with North-erton,[1] and uses it in his duel with Fitzpatrick. Altogether, then, the robbery and its result are not arbitrarily imposed on the narrative, but derive from certain pre-existent circumstances concerning Tom.

Yet despite all this the actual narration of the robbery retains much of the diagrammatic quality of its counterparts in *Joseph Andrews*. As in the earlier novel, the attack is introduced in mid-sentence, which minimizes the element of drama. And Tom's reaction—'Jones was at first somewhat shocked at this unexpected demand'—is inappropriately mild. This paragraph and the next—which concludes with Tom overpowering the highwayman—have an oddly unreal quality, and the reason seems to be Fielding's inadequate imaginative realization of the scene as a whole. He makes no attempt to describe the highwayman's approach to the complicated feat of holding up three horsemen with one pistol. Not for some time is it explained that Partridge has tried to flee, and has been thrown from his horse; while the whereabouts of the guide during the period remains vague. Fielding's use of indirect speech almost throughout the scene is typical of his undramatic approach to it.

What all this amounts to is that the level of reality in Fielding's account of the adventure is far lower than that of such passages as those quoted at the beginning of this section. There are two reasons for this disparity. One is Fielding's concern with exploiting the local potentialities of the incident. Just as he chooses, when describing the discovery of the infant Tom, to highlight the reactions of Mrs. Wilkins in the interests of making a mild satirical point, so here, as arbitrarily, he highlights those of Partridge. The pedagogue is shown in confident mood before the event:

' . . . for my own part, I never was less afraid in my life; for we are four of us, and if we all stand by one another, the best man in England

[1] Book vii, ch. 14; Henley ed., iv.46 ff.

can't rob us. Suppose he should have a pistol, he can kill but one of us, and a man can die but once—That's my comfort, a man can die but once.'[1]

During the engagement, however, he tries to flee, falls off his horse, and lies roaring for mercy. He afterwards excuses himself: '"A thousand naked men are nothing to one pistol; for though it is true it will kill but one at a single discharge, yet who can tell but that one may be himself?"'[2] This is a 'reversal' very similar to that which exposes the Patriot in *Joseph Andrews*.[3] Here there can be no very pungent satirical intention, since Partridge's total cowardice is already well established, but the change of front makes a pleasant comic point. It means, however, that Partridge's part in the incident has been predetermined by considerations other than those of drama and truth to life.

The other reason for the discrepancy in narrative convention is one that was of only minor importance in *Joseph Andrews*: Fielding's plot is too artificial for his material. In many parts of the novel, and particularly in the linking passages between episodes, he uses much realistic detail. But the episodes themselves cannot be realistically narrated, partly because they are too multifarious, partly because in almost every case certain elements must be subordinated in the interests of the points essential to Fielding's complex plot or his didactic theme.

In the highwayman scene attention is concentrated on Tom's conduct. He is civil to his attacker, but shows a calm determination, even though his life is in danger, not to give up Sophia's note. When he has overcome his assailant he rejects Partridge's demands that he kill him, but on the other hand he does not release him or give him money until he has probed the truth of his claims. It will be recalled that Fielding's Good-natured Man is characterized by 'a constant regard for desert'.

It is surely to concentrate on these various worthy reactions of Tom that Fielding has minimized the drama of the encounter. The last chapter suggested that certain incidents in *Joseph Andrews* seem no more than means to a didactic

---

[1] Henley ed., v.27.   [2] Henley ed., v.30.
[3] Book ii, ch. 9; Henley ed., i.156 ff.

end. The highwayman episode in *Tom Jones* is more plausibly related to the story as a whole, and serves a narrative as well as a didactic purpose, but its limited reality makes it appear similarly a mere means to an end.

Many of the episodes in *Tom Jones* are even more sketchily narrated. The 'childish incident' which shows 'a good-natured disposition in Tom Jones' is allotted a whole chapter, but the incident itself is disposed of in two sentences:

> The reader may remember that Mr. Allworthy gave Tom Jones a little horse, as a kind of smart-money for the punishment which he imagined he had suffered innocently.

> This horse Tom kept above half a year, and then rode him to a neighbouring fair, and sold him. (book iii, ch. 8)[1]

In Book IV Tom catches Sophia when she is thrown from her horse, and breaks his arm in the process.[2] It is afterwards accepted in the novel that he has saved her life at the risk of his own.[3] Yet both propositions seem unlikely. It is hard to imagine how Tom could have been killed in catching Sophia; in fact in the total absence of explanation by Fielding it is difficult to see how he could even have broken his arm. Later in the novel, moreoever, Sophia falls from her horse without suffering any kind of injury.[4] Fielding seems to be invoking the formula of the hero venturing his own life to save that of his lover, without inventing a convincing narrative embodiment of it.

Yet if these incidents are not retailed with much conviction, they at least produce appropriate narrative repercussions. Tom narrowly escapes chastisement for selling his horse, explains his reasons to Allworthy and is forgiven. The setting of Tom's broken arm is described, and he is afterwards shown as confined to bed for a period. Even the highwayman episode is given a suitable emphasis through the bulking out of the chapter with comment and moralizing. But there are some happenings necessary to the plot which are given almost no narrative weight at all. For

---

[1] Henley ed., iii.132.
[2] Chapter 13; Henley ed., iii.195.
[3] (e.g.) Book iv, ch. 13; book v, ch. 6; Henley ed., iii.196, 236.
[4] Book xi, ch. 2; Henley ed., iv.249.

instance the only reaction to Bridget Allworthy's death is that her brother drops 'a tender tear', and commits the funeral arrangements to Blifil.[1] Allworthy himself never alludes to his sister again, and Tom, who is elsewhere portrayed as above all a warm-hearted youth, shows no grief at all. The affair of Mrs. Hunt's proposal to Tom is introduced without any narrative preamble. Presumably he is supposed to know her quite well since she remarks in her letter that she has heard from the Millers 'that neither my person, understanding, or character are disagreeable to you',[2] but Fielding simply evades the task of developing this relationship within the narrative. Because he is relating the 'history' of Tom in terms of the events directly relevant to an elaborate plot, he naturally leaves a number of such gaps.

Fielding clearly borrows this plot from the artificial comedy, and he takes from the same source other features of technique equally formal. One of these is the stereotyping of reactions and dialogue. In moments of emotional crisis Sophia faints, or nearly faints;[3] when she and Tom are worried they 'pass sleepless nights';[4] Mrs. Miller 'falls to her knees'[5] to express gratitude or supplication. Partridge, bringing Tom the news of his 'incest': '... came stumbling into the room with his face paler than ashes, his eyes fixed in his head, his hair standing on end, and every limb trembling'.[6] Some emotions are formalized still more melodramatically. When Tom is first turned away by Allworthy he suffers a kind of frenzy: 'Here he presently fell into the most violent agonies, tearing his hair from his head, and using most other actions which generally accompany fits of madness, rage and despair.'[7] When he finds Sophia has left Upton without seeing him he falls on the wretched Partridge, who begs

[1] Book v, ch. 8; Henley ed., iii.250.

[2] Book xv, ch. 11; Henley ed., v.192.

[3] (e.g.) Book iv, ch. 14; book v. ch. 12; book vi, ch. 9; Henley ed., iii.197–8, 265, 306.

[4] (e.g.) Book v, ch. 3; book xiii, ch. 12; book xiv, ch. 3; Henley ed., iii.218; v.90, 101–2.

[5] (e.g.) Book xiv, ch. 6; book xvii, ch. 6; book xviii, ch. 8; Henley ed., v.121, 272, 336.

[6] Book xviii, ch. 2; Henley ed., v, 295.

[7] Book vi, ch. 12; Henley ed., iii.318.

for mercy: ' ... Jones, after staring wildly on him for a moment, quitted his hold, and discharged a rage on himself that, had it fallen on the other, would certainly have put an end to his being ... '[1] All these devices are ways of establishing that a character is adequately distressed, frightened, or otherwise moved by the situation in which the plot has involved him, without introducing distracting personal detail. Sometimes Fielding goes to the extreme of refusing to describe at all: 'What Sophia said, or did, or thought, upon this letter, how often she read it, or whether more than once, shall all be left to our reader's imagination.'[2]

Fielding's rhetorical dialogue also has a depersonalizing effect. At the climax of the book, for example, Tom's reconciliation with Allworthy has clearly to be of some intensity, yet for consistency's sake it cannot, alone of the emotional scenes, be interpreted realistically. Fielding therefore avoids portraying the beginning of the meeting: 'The first agonies of joy which were felt on both sides are indeed beyond my power to describe: I shall not therefore attempt it' (book xviii, ch. 10).[3] When direct speech is used it is highly rhetorical:

'O my dear uncle, this goodness, this tenderness overpowers, unmans, destroys me. I cannot bear the transports which flow so fast upon me. To be again restored to your presence, to your favor; to be once more thus kindly received by my great, my noble, my generous benefactor.' (book xviii, ch. 10)[4]

For Fielding the important thing is that Tom and Allworthy should be reunited with appropriate emotions and acknowledgements. Nuances of personal feeling are irrelevant to his purpose.

In *Joseph Andrews*, of course, serious speech and reactions had been similarly formalized. But there the hero and heroine were not taken too seriously, and emotional scenes were in any case few. In *Tom Jones*, however, Fielding has been at some pains to describe the love between Tom and Sophia from its minutest beginnings; it serves as a context

---

[1] Book xii, ch. 3; Henley ed., iv.309.
[2] Book xvi, ch. 3; Henley ed., v.212.
[3] Henley ed., v.345.   [4] Henley ed., v.345–6.

in which to judge the conduct of the pair. If the reality of their relationship is impaired by formal reactions and stilted address the novel loses much of its moral cogency. It is the problem of *The Modern Husband* all over again.

Ian Watt rightly suggests that *Tom Jones* exemplifies the principle that 'the importance of the plot is in inverse proportion to that of character'.[1] The action is constantly requiring various figures in the book to behave in a manner inconsistent with what has been revealed of their personalities. Tom, as hero, tends to be the principal victim. An interesting example of Fielding's failure to realize the effect of plot on characterization occurs in the fourth book. He accounts for Tom's early indifference to Sophia by explaining that he is already in love with Molly Seagrim. Tom feels a particular concern for Molly because he believes himself to be her first lover, and thinks he is responsible for her pregnancy. Not until he catches Square in her bedroom does he guess at her infidelity, his subsequent inquiries revealing further:

... that one Will Barnes, and not himself, had been the first seducer of Molly; and that the little child, which he had hitherto so certainly concluded to be his own, might very probably have an equal title, at least, to claim Barnes for its father. (book v, ch. 6)[2]

This allusion is the only evidence in the novel that Molly has in fact produced a child. Despite Tom's sense of obligation towards her, analysed at some length by Fielding, there is no hint of a concern for what he must assume to be his offspring. The actual birth has been allowed to pass without a reference. It might be added that it is chronologically almost certain that Molly initially succumbs to Square either in the last stages of pregnancy or the first weeks after childbirth.

The reason for this inconsistency is easily guessed. Molly has to be pregnant because it is through the physical fact of her pregnancy that Allworthy and thence Sophia learn of her affair with Tom. Once this aim has been achieved not only is Fielding no longer concerned with the incipient birth, he is obliged to play it down, since it will conflict with the

---

[1] *The Rise of the Novel*, p. 279.   [2] Henley ed., iii.232.

necessary intervention by Square, and generate a moral issue irrelevant in that Tom is to be providentially exculpated.

This is a significant lapse on Fielding's part because it blurs a moral issue about which he is trying to be particularly precise. There seems little point in his devoting, as he does, a whole chapter to Tom's mental struggle about his love for Sophia and his duty to Molly,[1] when the child, who would surely be a primary object of concern, is never mentioned.

There is a parallel suppression in the account of what has proved the most widely criticized of Tom's sins—his acceptance of money from Lady Bellaston. Fielding simply does not attempt to motivate this uncharacteristic action. He only makes the affair itself plausible by withholding, until well after the event, the fact that the lady is of advanced years and has bad breath.[2] This is surely another case where the demands of the plot have taken priority over conservation of character. It is Tom's financial obligations to his mistress which cause him to resort to a letter of mock-proposal to be rid of her. And it is Sophia's sight of this letter which leads to the renunciation of Tom required by the plot.

The problem is not quite the same with the minor characters, since Fielding borrows from stage convention not only the artificial plot but also the system of characterizing the lesser *dramatis personae* through 'humours'. This puts them on a quite separate moral level, so that their motives cannot be treated as seriously as those of the major characters.

It was submitted in the previous chapter that Fielding's discussion of Lady Booby's motives suggested a concern for conservation of character which might lead towards a new psychological realism. *Tom Jones* is filled with such passages of analysis: they take the form of direct description, soliloquy, personification, and ironic comment; yet somehow the total effect is not of a greatly increased insight. The reason

[1] Book v, ch. 3; Henley ed., iii.215 ff.
[2] Book xiii, ch. 9; Henley ed., v.74. There is no previous description of Lady Bellaston.

for this is the absolute moral distinction between central and peripheral characters which, it was pointed out in an earlier chapter, is the inevitable result of mixing romantic and 'humorous' conventions of portrayal. Partridge's fear of the highwayman, for instance, is purely comic: it is not set in the perspective which reveals Tom's conduct as courageous and generous. One of Partridge's humours (the characterization is a compound of several) is cowardice—Fielding does not have to justify each fresh instance of it. What 'humorous' characterization entails, in fact, is that characters are limited to one or two motives only.

The technique has its usefulness in a complex plot such as that of *Tom Jones*, since the eccentricity of a particular figure can often be made the motive for an unlikely action important to the story. Western, for example, is drawn from the pursuit of Sophia by the sight of a hunt;[1] his sister relaxes her severity when her vanity is applied to.[2] It also means, however, that these characters fall outside the moral system by which Fielding judges the conduct of Tom. It is revealed in the course of the narrative that Western is a fool and a sot, that he treated his wife like an unpaid servant,[3] and that his attitude towards his daughter's marriage is brutally wrong-headed. But since all these failings derive from a 'humorous' portrayal which is comic in intention, they are never adequately condemned. Western is freely forgiven by Tom, and soon becomes an idyllically happy grandfather. Sophia's cousin Harriet makes a rash marriage, and is at once abandoned by both her aunt and her uncle; but again Fielding avoids an assessment either of Harriet's moral responsibility in making the marriage and later deserting her husband, or of the Westerns' in rejecting her appeals for help. She is simply defined as promiscuous, being finally left living in well-paid sin, and hence exempt from both poverty and pity.

In such cases, of course, the plot requires that the character carries out certain actions—Western must insist on the marriage with Blifil; Harriet must betray Sophia's where-

---

[1] Book xii, ch. 2; Henley ed., iv.304 ff.
[2] Book xvii, ch. 4; Henley ed., v.262 ff.
[3] Book vii, ch. 4; Henley ed., iii.344 ff.

abouts to her aunt. Fielding is not concerned with their ethics. Certainly there have been novels in which the morality only of a selected character or characters was studied, with the rest of the cast relegated to mechanical status. In *Tom Jones*, however, Fielding seems unaware of any psychological distinction between his major figures and his minor ones, advancing incidental comments on various of the latter, which their limited potentiality makes it impossible for them to sustain. Mrs. Western, for example, is on one occasion described as 'a woman of a very extraordinary good and sweet disposition' with 'great affection for her brother, and still greater for her niece';[1] yet Fielding never has the chance to display these qualities in her, or indeed any outside the humours she embodies. Similarly, many of his passages of psychological analysis deal with the motives of characters as little open to moral alternatives as Black George and Sophia's maid, Honour. In such cases he invariably proves to be justifying an unlikely piece of behaviour, or making a comic point about human reasoning in general, rather than to be concerned with the ethical responsibility of the character in question. So that, while in theory he is expounding the motives of all his characters from a consistent narrative vantage-point, in fact he regards the majority of them as morally negligible, though he does not admit it. It is another aspect of the fact that *Tom Jones* is written on more than one level of reality.

3

It is a convenient over-simplification to suppose that *Tom Jones* was conceived in three stages. First Fielding decided on his moral theme, then he composed a story to illustrate it. Finally he incorporated all kinds of local incident and comment to reinforce both the narrative and the didactic interest.

The latter process is similar to that which had already produced the best of *Joseph Andrews*. This chapter has tried to show, among other things, that the moral scheme was an ambitious one, demanding a complex embodiment. But it

[1] Book vi, ch. 2; Henley ed., iii.279–80.

should also be emphasized how much Fielding's technique of story-telling contributes to the total effect of the novel. *Tom Jones* has been called 'the most lively book ever published'; and it is easy to see why. The story is told in a sequence of brief and immensely diversified episodes; the plot is full of twists and surprises; serious and comic are consciously alternated. Yet with all this the main end of the novel is never lost sight of. Fielding shows a control of pace and development far in advance of Richardson or even Marivaux. It is easy to undervalue all these qualities as being somehow independent of the literary stature of *Tom Jones*. But its remarkable readability is not unimportant or accidental; it stems from an elaborate and original technique for stimulating the reader's attention.

It cannot be denied, however, that the artificiality of this technique contrasts awkwardly with the realism of certain passages of the novel. In Fielding's lengthy description of Allworthy's house and estate,[1] for example, and of various minor details of the way of life there, he establishes a plausibly full context which he sometimes tries to draw upon; as when he describes Bridget Allworthy's growing fondness for Tom, which rouses the jealousy of Square,[2] or Tom's own relationship with Blifil: '. . . for Jones really loved him from his childhood, and had kept no secret from him, till his behaviour on the sickness of Mr. Allworthy had entirely alienated his heart . . . ' (book vi, ch. 7).[3] Yet these associations can never be substantiated in practice because of the arbitrary demands that the plot requires Fielding to make of his characters. The household can never become an imaginable entity because Allworthy's knowledge of Tom, or Tom's of Blifil, must never be made real enough to interfere with the pattern of deception on which the action is to depend. The characters have predestined roles, which the realism of their behaviour and relationships must not be allowed to impair.

It may be that Fielding himself sometimes felt the disparity of his methods. For instance he makes a rather

---

[1] Book i, ch. 4; Henley ed., iii.26–27.
[2] Book iii, ch. 6; Henley ed., iii.130.
[3] Henley ed., iii.299.

desperate effort to explain away Allworthy's tolerance of Thwackum:

> . . . for the reader is greatly mistaken if he conceives that Thwackum appeared to Mr. Allworthy in the same light as he doth to him in this history . . . Of readers who . . . condemn the wisdom or penetration of Mr. Allworthy, I shall not scruple to say that they make a very bad and ungrateful use of that knowledge which we have communicated to them. (book iii, ch. 5)[1]

This amounts to an admission that his comically exaggerated depiction of Thwackum disqualifies the character from any plausible relationship with the more realistically drawn Allworthy.

These inconsistencies not only reveal an important weakness in Fielding's narrative convention, they also help to limit the moral effectiveness of the book in several ways. First, a number of actions become less meaningful because of the diminished actuality of the context. At the simplest level, for example, Tom's generosity in giving the highwayman more than half his remaining small capital does not emerge very forcefully, because money is casually regarded throughout; none of the major characters is ever shown in hunger or want. Then, because of the different levels of characterization in the novel, the humane tolerance Fielding shows towards Nancy's pregnancy or Anderson's resort to highway robbery is never felt to be truly comprehensive. He insulates his hero and heroine from any such painful moral predicament. Finally, because he is sometimes obliged to be arbitrary about the motives of his leading character, the moral criteria he is proposing become blurred. The controversy about the 'corruptness' of the work, from the time of Dr. Johnson onwards, stems from the fact that Fielding's plot obliges him to make Tom perform actions inconsistent with his general role in the book's ethical scheme.

Tom Jones, then, is no more a coherent whole than *Joseph Andrews*. Its didactic and narrative excellences are not only independent of, but almost inconsistent with, one another. None the less it is difficult to see how Fielding could have projected his moral scheme in any other way than by means

[1] Henley ed., iii.125.

of the artificial plot. His concentration on Tom's morality shows up the helplessness of individual merit in the eighteenth-century social system. A more virtuous Tom who was merely the son of Jenny Jones could not have been rewarded by marriage with Sophia; a much wickeder Tom who was truly heir to the Allworthy estates, would have had her as a matter of course. The artificial plot is Fielding's means of bridging the gap between moral worth and material reward. It enables him to avoid answering the question that suggests itself so often in the course of the story: can he endorse a social system whose standards are not only irrelevant to the morality he is preaching, but often run counter to it? It is probably because his work as a magistrate compelled him to face this problem, that *Amelia* was to prove a much more sombre, cynical work, bitterly critical of many aspects of eighteenth-century society.

VIII

AMELIA

I N Book IV, chapter 3, of *Amelia*, after a conversation
between Mrs. Booth and her children, Fielding comments: 'This little dialogue, we are apprehensive, will be
read with contempt by many; indeed, we should not have
thought it worth recording was it not for the excellent
example which Amelia here gives to all mothers.'[1] Such
explanations confirm what the title of the novel suggests,
that its main didactic interest is to lie in the characterization
of the heroine. Amelia is the ideal wife and mother, and a
large part of Fielding's intention is to present her conduct,
shown to be admirable in a wide variety of difficult situations,
as an example to be followed.

As Sherburn has shown,[2] however, there is another
important didactic theme in *Amelia*. Booth, the hero, is
depicted as a deist, or even an atheist, his moral courage
sapped by his belief that men always act according to their
passions, and that their conduct can therefore have 'neither
merit nor demerit'. Sherburn claims: 'It was the psychological and moral task of the novel to rescue Booth from this
mental state.'[3] He connects this weakness in Booth with
yet a third theme, that of the corruptness of the aristocracy.
All the great men who appear in the novel are worthless and
self-interested. The Church, the Army, and the legal profession are all shown to be tainted with decadence.

Oddly enough, Sherburn does not quote Fielding's own
statement of his intentions in the dedicatory letter to Ralph
Allen: 'The following book is sincerely designed to promote
the cause of virtue, and to expose some of the most glaring
evils, as well public as private, which at present infest the

---

[1] Henley ed., iv.191.
[2] 'Fielding's *Amelia*: An Interpretation', *ELH*, iii (1936), 1–14.
[3] p. 7.

country . . . '¹ The first of these intentions recalls Fielding's claim in *Tom Jones* to be 'recommending goodness and innocence'. Clearly the conduct of Amelia, and possibly the conversion of Booth, is referred to, though in each case Fielding is going well beyond the mere demonstration of good-nature. The second aim, however, is a new one. Fielding's earlier writings had contained incidental comment on specific injustices, but only in *Amelia* does social reform become an important motive. A year previously *An Enquiry into the Causes of the Late Increase in Robbers* had been published,² and a year later appeared *A Proposal for Making an Effectual Provision for the Poor*.³ Clearly Fielding's work as a magistrate had made him more aware of flaws in the country's legal and social administration.

Since *Amelia* involves three major didactic themes it is not surprising to find that Fielding's theoretical ideas about narrative structure have to be subordinated. None the less the extent to which the standards outlined in *Joseph Andrews* and *Tom Jones* are neglected is fairly remarkable—sufficiently so to cast some doubt on the seriousness of the theorizing concerned. There are no introductory chapters, and many incidents have no connexion with the plot, which is in any case random and diffuse; the mock-heroic element has been altogether excluded, and the comi-prosai-epic has been practically stripped of comedy.

Apart from this, the subject-matter of *Amelia* suggests that Fielding is trying to write a new kind of narrative. The journey which plays so important a part in *Joseph Andrews* and *Tom Jones* is missing. Moreover, although the story is again about love, the hero and heroine are in this instance already married. Fielding seems almost to be discarding, then, two of the important ingredients of his previous novels—romantic interest and picaresque variety— choosing rather to rely on the intrinsic possibilities of material drawn from ordinary contemporary life. In conception at least, *Amelia* is far closer to being a realistic novel than either of its predecessors.

---

¹ Henley ed., vi.12.
² January 1751. *Amelia* appeared in December 1751.
³ January 1753.

Understandably, therefore, it presents new problems of construction. In each of the earlier books the hero's journey and, of course, his progress towards marriage, do much to provide development. *Amelia* lacks these obvious sources of continuity. The only external clue to Fielding's plans for controlling his new kind of material is the statement in *The Covent-Garden Journal* that his model had been Virgil.[1] Yet apart from the initial use of reminiscence to bring the story up to date there is little trace of this influence.[2] *Amelia* seems less to have been conditioned by the requirements of a theoretical narrative scheme than were either of the other novels.

I

Of the three main didactic themes in *Amelia* that of public corruption is the one which has most influence on the action of the story. The entire plot of the novel, from the time Booth leaves prison, derives from the fact that he cannot gain the deserved advancement which would rescue his family from their financial plight.

Booth is shown as having direct recourse to three influential acquaintances. His old friend Colonel James advises him to re-enter the Army, but soon becomes attracted to Booth's wife, and hence willing to serve him only in so far as it will assist his own chances of enjoying Amelia. Booth's other main hope, the Noble Lord, from the very beginning merely feigns a readiness to help, and merely because he, too, hopes to get Amelia into his power. Neither is in the least concerned with the merits of Booth, the sufferings of his family, or the needs of the Army. Moreover Fielding is careful to show that it would be an easy task for either of them to procure Booth a commission. The Noble Lord obtains one for Atkinson in twenty-four hours, when he is

---

[1] *The Covent-Garden Journal*, i.186.
[2] L. H. Powers lists a number of parallels in his article 'The Influence of the *Aeneid* on Fielding's *Amelia*', *MLN*, lxxi (1956), 330–6. Most of them are absurdly far-fetched. It does not seem to have been suggested that Booth's tour of the prison (book i, chs. 3 and 4; Henley ed., vi.22–24, and 26–31) might well be an ironic parody of Aeneas' trip to the underworld.

deceived into thinking that he will thereby gain favour with
Amelia; James gets places for two of his footmen within a
fortnight.[1]

Booth's last resource is the Great Man whom, on Bound's
advice, he bribes with the fifty pounds which Amelia has
scraped together at the cost of a visit to the pawnbroker.
The money is at once accepted, but there is again no intention of serving Booth. Fielding comments explicitly:

> Here I shall stop one moment, and so, perhaps, will my good-
> natured reader; for surely it must be a hard heart which is not affected
> with reflecting on the manner in which this poor little sum was raised,
> and on the manner in which it was bestowed. A worthy family, the
> wife and children of a man who had lost his blood abroad in the service
> of his country, parting with their little all, and exposed to cold and
> hunger, to pamper such a fellow as this!
>
> And if any such reader as I mention should happen to be in reality
> a great man, and in power, perhaps the horror of this picture may
> induce him to put a final end to this abominable practice of touching,
> as it is called; by which, indeed, a set of leeches are permitted to suck
> the blood of the brave and the indigent, of the widow and the orphan.
> (book xi, ch. 5)[2]

The ingenuous appeal in the second paragraph is evidence
of the directly reformative impulse behind *Amelia*. Nor does
it merely represent Fielding making didactic capital out of an
incident essential to his plot. The number of extraneous
examples of corruption in the novel show that the attack on
current methods of preferment is central to its purpose. An
old soldier named Bob Bound is introduced, for example,
described by Booth as 'one of the scandals of his country'.
After being commissioned by Marlborough 'for very particular merit' he has received no further promotion for thirty
years.[3] By contrast Sergeant Atkinson's commanding officer
is a boy of fifteen.[4] The case of Mrs. Bennet's first husband
shows that the injustice extends even to ecclesiastical preferment. A peer who was a friend at college betrays all his
promises of assistance; the Noble Lord pretends to interest

---

[1] Book xi, ch. 1; Henley ed., vii.244.
[2] Henley ed., vii.268.
[3] Book x, ch. 9; Henley ed., vii.236.
[4] Book iv, ch. 7; Henley ed., vi, 212.

himself in the young clergyman's affairs only in order to seduce the wife. In any event Dr. Harrison makes it clear that he regards the Church as partly responsible for the decadence of the country as a whole. In his argument with the young deacon he convicts a number of the clergy of avarice, ambition, and pride.

Altogether *Amelia* suggests an enormously widespread corruption among the country's leaders. Fielding does not hesitate to draw the pessimistic conclusion of his findings, his most explicit comment appearing in a chapter which provides yet another instance of administrative dishonesty. Dr. Harrison approaches a nobleman of his acquaintance on Booth's behalf, but the peer makes any assistance conditional on the doctor changing allegiances in a forthcoming election. In the argument that follows, the peer claims that Britain 'is as corrupt a nation as ever existed under the sun'. Dr. Harrison replies:

'If it be so corrupt . . . I think it is high time to amend it: or else it is easy to foresee that Roman and British liberty will have the same fate; for corruption in the body politic as naturally tends to dissolution as in the natural body.' (book xi, ch. 2)[1]

Short of condemning the system itself—an idea which never seems to occur to him—Fielding could hardly go further. Clearly the greatest of the 'glaring public evils' he had set himself to expose was the conduct of virtually all of society's leaders.

Fielding was justified in suggesting, as he does in this chapter, that Britain was on the verge of a total moral collapse, because he believed that the standards of a nation's rulers eventually influenced the conduct of the ordinary individual. This was by no means an idea peculiar to himself; Shaftesbury for instance, asserts:

THUS in *a civil* STATE or PUBLICK, we see that a virtuous Administration, and an equal and just Distribution of Rewards and Punishments, is of the highest service; not only by restraining the Vitious, and forcing them to act usefully to Society; but by making Virtue to be apparently the Interest of everyone . . . [2]

---

[1] Henley ed., vii.249.   [2] *Characteristicks*, London, 1733, ii.63.

9—T.R.

In his argument with the peer, Dr. Harrison puts forward a negative statement of the same view:

'Wherever true merit is liable to be superseded by favor and partiality, and men are intrusted with offices without any regards to capacity or integrity, the affairs of that state will always be in a deplorable situation . . . But, my lord, there is another mischief which attends this kind of injustice, and that is, it hath a manifest tendency to destroy all virtue and all ability among the people, by taking away all that encouragement and incentive which should promote emulation and raise men to aim at excelling in any art, science, or profession.' (book xi, ch. 2)[1]

Within the novel there is at least one example of an individual being corrupted by the decadence of society. James, who in Gibraltar is a devoted friend to Booth, in England devotes himself to the pursuit of Amelia. When discussing James's conduct with her Dr. Harrison declares:

'The nature of man is far from being in itself evil; it abounds with benevolence, charity, and pity . . . Bad education, bad habits, and bad customs, debauch our nature, and drive it headlong as it were into vice. The governors of the world, and I am afraid the priesthood, are answerable for the badness of it . . . I am convinced there are good stamina in the nature of this very man; for he hath done acts of friendship and generosity to your husband before he could have any evil design on your chastity; and in a Christian society, which I no more esteem this nation to be than I do any part of Turkey, I doubt not but this very colonel would have made a worthy and valuable member.' (book ix, ch. 5)[2]

It seems very likely that the moral uncertainty which Sherburn traces in Booth was intended by Fielding as a manifestation of a similar corruption of an individual. In first describing Booth as 'a freethinker—that is to say, a deist, or, perhaps, an atheist', Fielding attributes his outlook to the fact of his believing 'that a larger share of misfortunes had fallen to his lot than he had merited'.[3] Certainly Booth's experiences in seeking preferment show that he is living in a society where merit and reward bear little relation to one another. The essence of his moral position is that he dis-

---

[1] Henley ed., vii.250.   [2] Henley ed., vii.145.
[3] Book i, ch. 3; Henley ed., vi.25.

believes in 'religion and virtue' since he considers that men always act according to the dictates of their passions. His beliefs can only be confirmed by the self-interested conduct of the great men to whom he applies; at one point he answers Amelia's protests at the selfishness of the aristocracy by reminding her that everyone is bound by necessity, so that only if his ruling passion is benevolence can a man be generous.[1] He has some grounds for disbelieving in 'religion and virtue' since he sees their influence so seldom.

It may well be, then, that by the phrase 'as well public as private' Fielding was implying an endeavour to expose both the corruptness of the State and the effects of this corruption on the individual. It must be admitted that if this is the aim Fielding does not quite achieve it. Booth's scepticism is never satisfactorily shown to derive from the amorality of society; nor, despite Sherburn's reasonable inference, are his misdeeds shown to derive from his scepticism. His moral beliefs are referred to at regular intervals,[2] but they never become clearly operative in the action. Moreover it is nothing in his unfortunate experiences which eventually causes him to alter his views, but a chance reading of Barrow's sermons.[3] In fact the strongest reason for supposing that Fielding wished to establish a connexion between his hero's deism and the decadence of society's leaders is that without such a connexion Booth's moral theory seems no more than a pointless idiosyncrasy.

The uncertainty here is probably due to the fact that Booth's failure to obtain promotion renders him morally impotent. He is confined to the verge of the court, with no prospect of employment and no obvious course of action open to him. The lack of moral courage which Sherburn describes cannot, in these circumstances, be easily demonstrated.

The situation which obscures the nature of his weakness, however, serves to emphasize Amelia's moral strength.

[1] Book x, ch. 9; Henley ed., vii.237.
[2] (e.g.) Book i, ch. 3; book ii, ch. 2; book iii, chs. 4, 5; book vii, ch. 10; book x, ch. 9; book xii, ch. 5; Henley ed., vi.26, 71, 121, 127–8; vii.113–14, 237, 313.
[3] Book xii, ch. 5; Henley ed., vii.312–13.

Even before the story proper begins she has been shown in Booth's account of his past to be a woman of great worth. What first draws him to her is the courage with which she faces the prospect of permanent disfigurement after her nose has been broken in a coach accident.[1] As a wife she has been devoted and self-sacrificing, submitting to her husband's authority and tending him patiently when he is sick.[2]

It is in poverty, though, that her virtue is most clearly displayed. Faced with crises which dwarf anything that Sophia, for instance, has to bear, she remains undaunted. When Booth is unemployed she consoles him: '"Fear nothing, Billy; industry will always provide us a wholesome meal, and I will take care that neatness and cheerfulness shall make it a pleasant one"' (book iv, ch. 3).[3] When he incurs gambling debts, instead of upbraiding him, she pawns the last of her possessions to obtain the money. Towards the end of the book she contemplates total penury still indomitable:

'I am able to labor, and I am sure I am not ashamed of it . . . why should I complain of my hard fate while so many who are much poorer than I enjoy theirs? Am I of a superior rank of being to the wife of the honest laborer? am I not partaker of one common nature with her?' (book xii, ch. 8)[4]

Amelia's chastity is, of course, amply attested by her rejection of Bagillard, James, and the Noble Lord. She will not consider the faintest compromise even when it seems the only possible means of freeing her husband from prison.[5] The extent of her generosity is epitomized by her free forgiveness of Booth's affair with Miss Matthews. But in addition to these cardinal virtues Fielding shows her to exemplify all kinds of minor domestic excellences. He depicts her as a good mother and hostess, and shows her at work in the house:

As soon as the clock struck seven the good creature went down into the kitchen, and began to exercise her talents in cookery, of which she was a great mistress, as she was of every economical office from the

---

[1] Book ii, ch. 1; Henley ed., vi.66.
[2] Book iii, ch. 7; Henley ed., vi.134.   [3] Henley ed., vi. 185.
[4] Henley ed., vii, 333.   [5] Book viii, ch. 3; Henley ed., vii.74-5.

highest to the lowest; and as no woman could outshine her in a drawing-room, so none could make the drawing-room itself shine brighter than Amelia. And, if I may speak a bold truth, I question whether it be possible to view this fine creature in a more amiable light than while she was dressing her husband's supper, with her little children playing round her. (book xi, ch. 8)[1]

One of Fielding's main methods of 'promoting the cause of virtue' in *Amelia* was obviously to be a demonstration of true womanly goodness. By exposing his heroine to poverty he is able to show her nobility in a variety of trying situations from which she would be protected by the possession of money.

There are also several clearly defined subsidiary themes in the novel. Fielding widens the scope of his comment on female conduct through the insertion of the stories of Miss Matthews and Mrs. Atkinson. The first of these shows how immorality, the second how even a small compromise, can betray a woman into ruin: by contrast, of course, Amelia's virtue shines the brighter. The heinousness of adultery is another point the author labours. Dr. Harrison, for instance, is twice made to hint[2] at the view later advanced in *The Covent-Garden Journal*,[3] that adultery should be made punishable by law. Finally there is an insistence that morality has no connexion with class. Booth affirms early in the book:

'As it is no rare thing to see instances which degrade human nature in persons of the highest birth and education, so I apprehend that examples of whatever is really great and good have been sometimes found amongst those who have wanted all such advantages. In reality, palaces, I make no doubt, do sometimes contain nothing but dreariness and darkness, and the sun of righteousness hath shone forth with all its glory in a cottage.' (book iii, ch. 7)[4]

Plainly this idea is focused in the characterization of Atkinson. His worthy behaviour and the purity of his silent love for Amelia are implicitly, and at one point explicitly, contrasted to the hypocrisy and lust of James and the Noble

---

[1] Henley ed., vii, 282–3.
[2] Book ix, ch. 5; book x, ch. 2; Henley ed., vii.145, 189.
[3] *The Covent-Garden Journal*, ii.114 ff.   [4] Henley ed., vi.139.

Lord. When Atkinson, on what he thinks to be his death-bed, reveals to his foster-sister his secret devotion to her, she is understandably moved:

> To say the truth, without any injury to her chastity, that heart, which had stood firm as a rock to all the attacks of title and equipage, of finery and flattery, and which all the treasures of the universe could not have purchased, was yet a little softened by the plain, honest, modest, involuntary, delicate, heroic passion of this poor and humble swain; for whom, in spite of herself, she felt a momentary tenderness and complacency, at which Booth, if he had known it, would perhaps have been displeased. (book xi, ch. 6)[1]

Since the story has so heavy a didactic load to carry, it is not surprising that its structure should be subject to strain. Narrative interest is sustained by an arbitrary alternation of hope and fear concerning Booth's financial prospects and Amelia's chances of surviving the numerous attempts on her virtue. There is nothing to parallel the elaborate relation of incident to plot in *Tom Jones*. Fielding's complex of didactic purposes compels him to resort to a loose-leaf technique rather similar to that of *Joseph Andrews*, many characters and incidents having no narrative function what-soever. Miss Matthews's story, for instance, which occupies much of the first book, is largely dispensable, and so is that of Mrs. Atkinson, which takes up nearly the whole of the seventh. Dr. Harrison's titled friend is introduced only for the purposes of the discussion on aristocratic decadence,[2] and the young deacon only for the long disputes about charity and the morality of the clergy.[3] In another gratuitous chapter Fielding makes Booth advance various literary views, and attack the current system of literary patronage.[4] He also finds occasion to canvass a number of specific legal issues. The chapter which describes Booth's prosecution of Betty[5] can have no other motive than to call attention to an anomalous law of theft. Elsewhere Fielding attacks the law

---

[1] Henley ed., vii.275–6.

[2] Book xi, ch. 2; Henley ed., vii.244 ff.

[3] Book xi, chs. 8, 10; Henley ed., vii.160 ff. and 173 ff.

[4] Book viii, chs. 5–6; Henley ed., vii. 83 ff. The episode extends into the beginning of the next chapter, p. 91.

[5] Book xi, ch. 7; Henley ed., vii.276 ff.

of perjury,[1] the practice of imprisonment for non-payment of legal fees,[2] the powers of bailiffs,[3] the law of evidence,[4] and the conditions affecting the granting of a search warrant.[5] Such demonstrations of particular weaknesses in the legal machinery are important to Fielding's didactic intention, but they are often embodied in incidents unrelated to the main story. There are signs that the author himself was aware of the dangers of irrelevance. In the 'trial' of *Amelia* in *The Covent-Garden Journal* the prosecution suggest 'That the Scene of the Gaol is *low and unmeaning*, and brought in by Head and Shoulders, without any Reason, or Design'.[6] The first edition of the novel contains a chapter in which Booth's little daughter contracts a fever, and after sinking fast under the ministrations of an ignorant physician and apothecary, is finally cured by the real-life Dr. Thompson, who is not recognized by the medical profession. Fielding concludes the episode: 'Some readers will, perhaps, think this whole chapter might have been omitted; but though it contains no great matter of amusement, it may at least serve to inform posterity concerning the present state of physic' (book iv, ch. 10).[7] He removed the chapter when revising *Amelia*. Clearly he had inserted it only to puff Dr. Thompson and to make an opportunity for his customary satire against the medical profession.

As usual he moralizes both directly and indirectly throughout the course of the book; but there are some interesting departures from previous practice. His own comments totally lack the light-heartedness of those in *Joseph Andrews* and *Tom Jones*. Gone almost completely are the ironic equivocations and the self-deprecating manner; Fielding is oracularly direct:

Here, reader, give me leave to stop a minute, to lament that so few are to be found of this benign disposition; that, while wantonness, vanity, avarice, and ambition are every day rioting and triumphing

---

[1] Book i, ch. 4; Henley ed., vi.28.
[2] Book i, ch. 4; Henley ed., vi.29.
[3] Book xii, ch. 5; Henley ed., vii.315–16.
[4] Book xi, ch. 3; Henley ed., vii.256.
[5] Book xii, ch. 7; Henley ed., vii.327–8.
[6] *The Covent-Garden Journal*, i.179.   [7] Henley ed., vi.232.

in the follies and weakness, the ruin and desolation of mankind, scarce one man in a thousand is capable of tasting the happiness of others. (book iv, ch. 4)[1]

The moralizing by characters in the book tends to be equally severe. Dr. Harrison is far blunter than Allworthy, in both the manner and the matter of his discourse. He threatens Colonel Bath with damnation,[2] and on one occasion even reduces Amelia to tears.[3] His lectures to the young deacon are typical of his uncompromising style. Concerning the ambitious cleric he asks rhetorically:

'Must he not himself think, if ever he reflects at all, that so glorious a Master will disdain and disown a servant who is the dutiful tool of a court-favorite, and employed either as the pimp of his pleasure, or sometimes, perhaps, made a dirty channel to assist in the conveyance of that corruption which is clogging up and destroying the very vitals of his country?' (book ix, ch. 10)[4]

The greater seriousness of theme and tone is reinforced by a greater seriousness of incident. Besides the breaking of Amelia's nose, there are Booth's injuries and illness at Gibraltar, the death of his sister, the shipwreck, and the drowning of Mrs. Atkinson's mother. These all contribute to a total picture much more sombre than that presented by either of the two previous novels. Fittingly there are no mock-heroics in the novel, and virtually no comic incidents. Altogether the pessimistic implications of Fielding's didactic themes gain credit from his new willingness to admit the more painful contingencies of ordinary life.

2

The characterization of Atkinson and James provides a useful index to the increased realism of *Amelia*. In their general role as friends of the Booths they represent a new departure for Fielding. Joseph Andrews and Tom Jones had been depicted almost as solitaries. It is true that Tom eventually becomes intimate with Nightingale, but for the first twenty years of his life he apparently lacks even an

---

[1] Henley ed., vi.194–5.   [2] Book ix, ch. 3; Henley ed., vii.134.
[3] Book ix, ch. 4; Henley ed., vii.142.   [4] Henley ed., vii.176.

acquaintance of the same age and sex, except for the wretched Blifil. The friendlessness of his heroes is one aspect of Fielding's comparative neglect of social context in his first two novels. To a great extent he isolates his leading characters—most obviously, of course, by setting them on the road—so that their adventures take place in a kind of vacuum. In *Amelia*, however, hero and heroine are given a much fuller social definition. They are a married couple with three children, compelled by debt to take lodgings within the verge of the court. Booth is a half-pay subaltern and his wife a busy housekeeper. James and Atkinson are only two of a circle of friends from all walks of life, with whom they are in regular contact.

This careful 'placing' of the Booths adds greatly to the verisimilitude of the story. In the two previous novels the lack of background had conveniently limited the repercussions of any one incident. The episodes were so varied and prolific that Fielding would have been greatly embarrassed to depict them producing the consequences which would have ensued in real life. None the less, the reality of the story was impaired in that without this contextual perspective action tended to be weakly defined. In *Amelia* there can be no such stratification of incident, since the central characters are closely involved with a stable environment. If Booth is taken by the bailiffs the children cry and have to be comforted; if Amelia quarrels with Mrs. Ellison the family is obliged to change house.

The part played by James in the novel has a further interest. It was shown earlier in this chapter that he is explicitly an example of a worthy man corrupted by society. As such, he is a kind of character new in Fielding's work: a genuine mixture of good and bad. Fielding had often before claimed to be portraying such a figure, but in practice had only produced such characters as Diana Western, whose better qualities are mentioned but never exemplified, and Mrs. Waters, whose moral position is not really taken seriously. The nearest approach to such a mixed personality in the earlier novels is Tom Jones himself, and Fielding makes it clear that he regards his misdeeds, though real enough, as relatively minor: Tom never sins against Good-nature.

James, however, is thoroughly good at one juncture, and thoroughly evil at another; and there are other characters in the novel of similar moral complexity. Amelia's saviour, Mrs. Atkinson, is willing to compromise herself to some extent to gain a commission for her husband. Booth himself, in addition to his agnosticism, and his real guilt in the affair with Miss Matthews, is shown to have an inveterate weakness for gaming. On the other hand Trent, the pimp of the Noble Lord, has been a gallant soldier,[1] and even Mrs. Ellison is allowed a certain generosity.[2] Altogether *Amelia* shows a new degree of moral realism.

Atkinson is significant as being the first proletarian in Fielding's work to be given true dignity. In *Joseph Andrews* and *Tom Jones* the author's moral views were clearly conditioned by social preconceptions: Joseph and Fanny were virtuous, but they were patronized. The morality of the lower classes was not treated with the same seriousness as that of, say, Sophia. In a novel concerned with ethical fundamentals this was a severe limitation. Only in *Amelia* does Fielding come near to an objective moral view of society.

Since James and Atkinson are developed characters in their own right as well as being friends of the Booths, they represent yet another new departure in Fielding's narrative technique. The artificial comedy scheme, whereby the *dramatis personae* are divided into a small group of 'serious' characters, and a larger group of 'humorous' minor characters, has been almost abandoned. In *Tom Jones* not only were the leading figures friendless, but those characters who did surround them were nearly all comic puppets. Even Sophia's father and Tom's mother were made respectively booby-squire and prude. In *Amelia*, for the first time, there are several supporting characters drawn 'in the round'. The absolute moral and emotional distinction between major and minor figures has been largely removed.

All these factors contribute to the fabrication of a context which has much of the complexity of real life. Each character has a distinct relationship with the other characters, and

---

[1] Book xi, ch. 3; Henley ed., vii.256.
[2] Book vii, chs. 8, 9; Henley ed., vii.51, 57.

these relationships evolve in the course of the story. Atkinson marries Mrs. Bennet; Colonel James pursues and eventually possesses Miss Matthews; his wife is attracted to Booth, but soon gives up hope of winning him. This pattern of inter-involvement makes the sequence of encounters which Fielding exhibits far more psychologically intricate than anything in his first two novels. In the dialogue between Colonel James and Atkinson, for instance,[1] all that passes is conditioned by the colonel's hope of converting Atkinson into a pimp for obtaining Amelia's favours, and by the sergeant's own secret passion for his foster-sister. The discussion between the Booths and Dr. Harrison about the advisability of Amelia's accompanying her husband to the West Indies,[2] has as an undercurrent her knowledge that James wishes to keep her in England in order to seduce her. When Booth, later in the story, fiercely accuses his wife of having concealed James's advances, the real cause of his anger is shame at having lost fifty pounds at play. The chapter concludes: 'Thus the husband and wife became again reconciled, and poor Amelia generously forgave a passion of which the sagacious reader is better acquainted with the real cause than was that unhappy lady' (book x, ch. 6).[3] For the first time Fielding is making his dialogues reveal far more than is actually expressed.

The greater emphasis on social context in *Amelia* demands an increased amount of minor realistic detail. There are the dialogues with the children, for example, and the usual references to food and drink, which have more than the usual relevance in view of Amelia's domestic proclivities. Early in the novel the Booths are seen lunching on scrag of mutton;[4] on the night of her husband's final assignation with Miss Matthews Amelia has prepared his favourite meal, 'a fowl and egg sauce and mutton broth'.[5] The Booths meet few notable adventures and their pleasures are simple ones: a few visits, a trip to Vauxhall. Fielding des-

[1] Book viii, ch. 8; Henley ed., vii,100 ff.
[2] Book ix, ch. 4; Henley ed., vii.139 ff.
[3] Henley ed., vii.219.
[4] Book v, ch. 2; Henley ed., vi.234.
[5] Book xi, ch. 8; Henley ed., vii.282.

cribes how they pass an evening at home after a call from Mrs. James:

> Booth and his wife, the moment their companion was gone, sat down to supper on a piece of cold meat, the remains of their dinner. After which, over a pint of wine, they entertained themselves for a while with the ridiculous behaviour of their visitant. But Amelia, declaring she rather saw her as the object of pity than anger, turned the discourse to pleasanter topics. The little actions of their children, the former scenes and future prospects of their life, furnished them with many pleasant ideas; and the contemplation of Amelia's recovery threw Booth into raptures. At length they retired, happy in each other. (book iv, ch. 6)[1]

In such passages as this, consisting of small particulars irrelevant to the main story, Fielding sugests the daily routine surrounding the central events he has chosen to describe. Unlike Tom Jones or Joseph Andrews, the Booths have a way of life.

It would be possible to adduce numerous circumstances which contribute to this sense of actuality. Dr. Harrison's mode of speech is one example. Many critics have found his pedantic humour rather tiresome, but in fact it represents Fielding's first attempt to characterize a figure through a conversational habit not intrinsically comic.

The kind of force such minor details can be given is well illustrated by the description of Amelia's lonely evening at home when her husband is out gambling:

> At ten then she sat down to supper by herself, for Mrs. Atkinson was then abroad. And here we cannot help relating a little incident, however trivial it may appear to some. Having sat some time alone, reflecting on their distressed situation, her spirits grew very low; and she was once or twice going to ring the bell to send her maid for half a pint of white wine, but checked her inclination in order to save the little sum of sixpence, which she did the more resolutely as she had before refused to gratify her children with tarts for their supper from the same motive. And this self-denial she was very probably practising to save sixpence, while her husband was paying a debt of several guineas incurred by the ace of trumps being in the hands of his adversary. (book x, ch. 5)[2]

---

[1] Henley ed., vi.208. [2] Henley ed., vii.214.

This brief description defines exactly the extent of Booth's folly in being drawn into gambling. He is squandering guineas at a time when his family must think in terms of pennies. For the first time in Fielding's novels money takes on real value; in *Joseph Andrews* and *Tom Jones*, the facility with which it is given, stolen, lost, and found, reduces it to a meaningless commodity. The Booths' financial plight can eventually be stated quite exactly by Amelia: '"... I believe all we have in the world besides our bare necessary apparel would produce about sixty pounds ..."' (book x, ch. 6).[1]

The realistic detail, then, though not often as directly as in the instance quoted above, helps to supply moral definition. Amelia's devotion during her husband's illness carries more weight because he is convincingly sick, spitting blood and subject to 'violent sweats',[2] not suffering from the nominal disease of an Allworthy. Similarly, if on a rather different level, Booth's infidelity to Amelia seems appropriately sinful because of the contrast provided by her own resolute chastity and Atkinson's selfless devotion. In both large ways and small the realistic context gives meaning to Fielding's moral adjurations.

To praise the greater realism of *Amelia*, then, is not to imply that this kind of writing is in some absolute sense especially commendable. It is proper to this particular novel because essential to a full realization of the book's didactic purpose. If the total effect is at all confused, it is because a number of artificial elements have survived. The plot depends on the usual coincidences and deceptions: Booth has critically important re-encounters with three old acquaintances, Miss Matthews, Colonel James, and Atkinson, in each case purely by chance; Dr. Harrison is led to prosecute him through a misunderstanding; four characters in the book—Hebbers, Bagillard, Atkinson, and Robinson —are brought to the brink of death in order to precipitate some narrative issue, and afterwards revived. There are even episodes which derive straight from the comedy of intrigue: the deceits of the masquerade, for example, and Booth's entry into Mrs. Harris's house concealed in a wine-hamper.

[1] Henley ed., vii.216.
[2] Book iii, chs. 5, 7; Henley ed., vi.129, 134.

Above all, of course, it is only through a laborious 'discovery', similar to that in *The Temple Beau*, that the Booths' difficulties are finally resolved.

The Virgilian convention by which the chief characters bring their own histories up to date is also discordantly artificial. Booth, for instance, produces relevant letters which he happens to have in his pocket-book, and several times pauses in his account to explain away his unlikely feats of memory and mimicry.[1]

But the most limiting convention in the novel is that governing the characters' speech and reactions in moments of emotion; they are as crudely formalized as those in *Tom Jones*:

> 'Thou heavenly angel! thou comfort of my soul!' cried Booth, tenderly embracing her; then starting a little from her arms, and looking with eager fondness in her eyes, he said, 'Let me survey thee; art thou really human, or art thou not rather an angel in human form? O no!' cried he, flying again into her arms, 'thou art my dearest woman, my best, my beloved wife.' (book x, ch. 6)[2]

Since the harshness of the story demands that the Booths face a regular series of misfortunes, such stylized reactions are invoked again and again. 'O Heavens!', repeated at every crisis, gradually loses all force; Amelia faints five times and Miss Matthews twice, while Mrs. Atkinson has convulsions; Booth sheds tears on some ten occasions. Altogether the realism of context and incident in *Amelia* cruelly exposes the lack of any available technique for dramatizing strong emotions convincingly.

There are a number of miscellaneous factors which also diminish the actuality of the novel. One is Fielding's readiness to insert extraneous didactic matter even at the expense of narrative harmony. The chapter in which Booth airs his literary views in the bailiff's house makes him appear inappropriately cheerful; that where he pursues Betty inappropriately cruel. Similarly unrealistic are many of the purely emotional passages in the story. Fielding hints at the new trend in his dedication: 'The good-natured reader, if

---

[1] Henley ed. (e.g.), vi.72, 90, 111, 135, 154.
[2] Henley ed., vii.215–16.

his heart should be here affected, will be inclined to pardon many faults for the pleasure he will receive from a tender sensation ... '[1] Clearly the growing cult of sentimentalism was having its influence. In *Tom Jones* there had been traces of such a tendency, and even 'A chapter which, thought short, may draw tears from some eyes',[2] but little conscious striving after pathos. *Amelia*, however, contains a number of scenes, such as that of Booth's parting from his wife on leaving for Gibraltar,[3] which strive for effect through inflated expressions of feeling, and are thus false to the emotional realism of the book as a whole.

Fielding's moral objectivity seems slightly compromised too, in that his attitude to certain of his characters is still affected by social preconceptions. For instance Murphy, who forges the will giving Amelia's estates to her sister, is hanged; but Miss Harris herself, the instigator and main beneficiary, is allowed to escape to France and given a small income. Atkinson, who emerges in the story as a much nobler figure than Booth, is rewarded only by a reasonably happy marriage with Mrs. Bennet, the quick-tempered blue-stocking.

The considerable realism of *Amelia*, then, is not sustained in every aspect of the work. Fielding is still hampered, even though unconsciously, by various moral and literary conventions of his time inconsistent with the kind of story he is clearly trying to relate.

3

There is a variety of possible reasons why *Amelia* remains the least regarded of Fielding's novels. Certainly it lacks the gaiety of its two predecessors, but this would count for less if it had fully accomplished its author's serious intentions. Of the three main themes outlined earlier in this chapter only that of Amelia's virtue is adequately realized; though insipid for some tastes she has never lacked admirers. The other two themes make little impact. Booth's moral uncertainty is never expressed in action, and the final abrupt

[1] Henley ed., vi.12.   [2] Book xiii, ch. 10; Henley ed., v.77.
[3] Book iii, ch. 2; Henley ed., vi.111 ff.

conversion is rendered undemonstrable and largely unnecessary by his subsequent change of fortune. The corruption Fielding was attacking was of a kind particular to his
own time, so that his exposures rather lack force today.
Moreover, as Sherburn points out, he evades the full implications of the situation he describes by arbitrarily imposing a
happy ending.

This glib economic solution enables Fielding to beg most
of the moral questions he has been concerned to raise in his
novel. *Amelia*, as usual, is a story of love and money, but in
this case it seems that the money will have somehow to be
earned. Having demonstrated, however, that contemporary
society is too corrupt for a 'gentleman' to be able to make an
honest living, Fielding is content merely to provide a conventional escape for his particular hero. Early in the book he
shows an old man unjustly dying in prison;[1] but he reserves
such bleak objectivity for the margin of his story. Since
Amelia survives unscathed where Mrs. Bennet did not,
there is even an unrealistic suggestion that perfect virtue is
unassailable. The ethics of self-preservation in a corrupt
society are left unclear. Amelia is contemptuous of the ruse
by which Mrs. Atkinson wins a commission for her husband,
but Booth's own experience shows the futility of relying on
merit for preferment. Is it legitimate to cheat the corrupt?
Fielding's negative answer is a facile one, and the retirement
of the Booths into the country represents an admission of
defeat. The best the individual can hope for is to have
enough money to be able to preserve his virtue away from
society.

Amelia makes it clear that Fielding now saw the social
system which he automatically accepted, to be in an advanced stage of moral decay. It is not surprising, therefore,
that despite its happy ending the novel shows an extreme
pessimism. Character after character seems worthy but
proves treacherous: the Noble Lord, for example, Robinson,
James, Mrs. James, Miss Matthews, Mrs. Ellison, and even
Betty the maid. Booth's fellow officers in Gibraltar refuse to
help him when he is in financial need; his fellow farmers
systematically bankrupt him. Much of the incident is

[1] Book i, ch. 4; Henley ed., vi.27–28.

sombre: Booth's tour of the prison, the shipwreck,[1] the trip
to Vauxhall with its unhappy outcome,[2] the gratuitously
wretched deaths of Booth's sister and Mrs. Atkinson's
mother.[3] The conclusion of the story is suitably gloomy.
Colonel Bath has been killed in a duel, Mrs. Ellison has
died of drink and the Noble Lord of venereal disease, 'by
which he was at last become so rotten that he stunk above
ground'; Amelia's sister has also 'died in a most miserable
manner', and Robinson, of whose amendment Dr. Harrison
had high hopes,[4] has relapsed into crime and been hanged.
The total effect of *Amelia* is undeniably depressing.

There is a good deal of clumsiness both in the construction
and in the telling of the story. Fielding's use of an artificial
ending means that his hero, Booth, can do nothing to help
himself, and that there is no crisis for the action to work
towards. The insertion of incidents solely for didactic
purposes gives the narrative a fragmentary quality. Moreover the centre of gravity of the novel is uncertain. The book
gets under way with the story of Miss Matthews who, it
unexpectedly transpires, is to play only a very minor part
in the events to follow. Later the focus of interest is constantly shifted from Booth's preferment to Amelia's virtue
and back again. These vacillations contribute to the dis-
jointed quality of the work.

All these factors are relevant to the frequent under-
estimation of *Amelia*. But Dr. Johnson was probably near the
mark in ascribing the short-term failure of the novel to
Amelia's broken nose. She was the first heroine in English
fiction allowed far enough out of the glass-case of idealism
to injure her beauty. Compromised as was Fielding's realism in many respects, it was far too much for most of his
contemporaries. In the 'trial' of the book in *The Covent-
Garden Journal* the burden of the prosecution case is the
repeated charge that *Amelia* is 'low'. Counsellor Town asks
the Censor to: '. . . pass such a Sentence as may be a dreadful
Example to all future Books, how they dare stand up in

---

[1] Book iii, ch. 4; Henley ed., vi.121–5.
[2] Book ix, ch. 9; Henley ed., vii.166 ff.
[3] Book ii, ch. 4 and book vii, ch. 2; Henley ed., vi.82–83 and vii.13.
[4] Book xii, ch. 8; Henley ed., vii. 337.

Opposition to the Humour of the Age.'[1] Fielding had estimated very accurately the reasons for the unpopularity of his story. In trying, about a century too soon, to write a realistic, socially-reformative novel, he was not only straining the formal literary machine beyond its powers: he was ensuring incomprehension and commercial failure.

[1] *The Covent-Garden Journal,* i.179.

IX

CONCLUSION

ONE object of this book has been to demonstrate that many of Fielding's chosen narrative techniques were incompatible. Various specific incongruities have been pointed out by means of close analysis. In concluding it seems necessary to try to answer a question arising out of these analyses but only touched on in the preceding chapters: how important is this kind of discrepancy to the overall success or failure of the novels?

It seems safer to talk about one particular case than to generalize, and *Tom Jones* seems the obvious choice. Of this book Ian Watt remarks: ' . . . [it] is only part novel, and there is much else—picaresque tale, comic drama and occasional essay'.[1] In its context Professor Watt's comment is narrower in scope than is apparent here. He has proposed that the lowest common denominator of the novel as a genre is the observance of 'formal realism', and he has shown how often Fielding departs from this standard. But it is surprising, after all, that the diagnosis is not true in a general way, as well as in Watt's special sense. The various component techniques he mentions do frequently retain too much of their intrinsic character to blend smoothly into the narrative as a whole. Yet although there are passages, and even whole episodes, which stand out awkwardly, there can be no doubt that Fielding's diverse methods do harmonize sufficiently to produce an effect as a totality. *Tom Jones* may be only 'part novel' in terms of formal realism, but generally speaking readers and critics have always reacted to it as to an integrated whole, and not as to a collection of amusing parts.

Moreover despite the many artificial aspects of the work this overall effect is realistic rather than otherwise. *Tom Jones* has always been read as a novel, not as a moral fable. Fielding

[1] *The Rise of the Novel*, p. 288.

scholars who carefully classify and analyse the various characteristics of Tom and Sophia are only rationalizing the reactions of the ordinary reader. The book is close enough to reality for the critic to think it reasonable to accuse Tom of hypocrisy for lecturing Nightingale on sexual morality, or Allworthy of gullibility for believing Blifil's lies. And this way of looking at the novel seems to answer to Fielding's own concepts. In the course of his brief career as a novelist he learns to discard many of his more formal devices— soliloquy for instance, and mock-heroic descriptions—and to develop the realistic aspects of his stories.

At first sight this seems to be the end of the inquiry. Fielding may have mixed his narrative methods, but thanks to some mysterious process of artistic fusion a unified result emerges. Ultimately, however, this is not a satisfactory conclusion. The total effect produced, it seems, tends towards realism. But in that case what has happened to the artificial features of the novel? They are so numerous that they must surely play some part in conditioning the reader's response. How does so heterogeneous a work as *Tom Jones* come to be construed as a coherent whole? And what kind of whole does the average reader think he is accepting?

These questions would be easier to answer if more were known about the way in which novels in general make their effect. Theoretical discussion of the genre has traditionally tended to rely on detailed analysis of separate elements: characters, plot and so on. The unstated assumption is that such analysis will amplify and elucidate the general impression gained by the intelligent reader. Indeed this is an inescapable belief if discussion of the novel is to be possible at all, for the general impression itself is by definition immune from close examination. If scrutinized it ceases to be a general impression. The critic's only resource seems to be to study what gave rise to it.

But there is none the less a clear and important difference between the impression the novel produces as a whole, and the sum total of the effects it yields up to analysis. A novel is a symposium of extraordinarily diverse information, but it is not to be judged merely on the quality of this information. The major distinction between the novel and the picaresque tale is that the information provided by the former coalesces into a credible picture of real life. But the novel is a fluid genre, which has always been in some sense experimental. No author can be certain in advance that a given detail of his narrative is going to 'take'. Not even the accepted masterpieces of the genre are wholly devoid of arbitrary or random elements. Certain words, or paragraphs, or even whole chapters, could be omitted without apparent loss, in that they do not contribute to the effect made by the narrative as a whole. A novel, in other words, is both more and less than the sum total of its parts.

This point is of particular relevance to a consideration of *Tom Jones*—or any of Fielding's novels—because, as this study has tried to show, the relationship of the part to the whole here is unorthodox by modern standards. The contemporary reader, or even critic, assumes that a novel is primarily intended as a picture of real life, and that virtually all the information provided by the author will have been included with reference to this intention. But in the case of *Tom Jones* the choice of episodes was governed by no such principle. Many of the incidents which embody specific moral points have almost no relevance to the picture of life emerging from the story proper. The traditional method of analysis therefore leads to misconstruction. It will interpret as important to the effect produced by the narrative as a whole all kinds of detail deriving solely from some local purpose. For instance Allworthy has been described as a prig because of his sententious addresses to Jenny and to Dr. Blifil. Yet these speeches are included not to demonstrate an aspect of Allworthy's character, but to instruct the reader. Again, the account of Bridget Allworthy's life with her husband is designed not to show what kind of person she is, but to satirize a certain type of marriage which Fielding thought to be deplorably prevalent.

Naturally the difference between Fielding's practice here and that of the modern novelist is only one of degree. Allworthy has to be shown as a character capable of sermonizing, and his sister as a woman capable of suppressed lust and domestic hatred. But whereas the modern writer would feel constrained to root such striking tendencies deep in the characterization as a whole, Fielding is content simply to leave the Allworthys weakly and generally defined—he as a Good Man and she as a Prude—and manipulate them in different ways for a variety of local purposes.

In the chapter on *Tom Jones* a second way was noted in which an individual episode may provide information use-less, or even misleading, from the point of view of the narrative as a whole, Fielding is sometimes cornered by his plot. Allworthy's belief that he is about to die (Book V, Chapter 7), for example, is not remotely intended to imply that he is a hypochondriac. Such return-trips to the brink of death are frequently arranged by Fielding to advance his plot. Similarly, Bridget's apparent transfer of affection from Square to Tom (Book III, Chapter 6) is not significant of anything in any of their characters—it is simply included to explain the otherwise unaccountable fact that Thwackum and Square, who are at variance on every other topic, happen to be united in hatred towards Tom.

On the other hand some of the information which Field-ing provides solely to enhance the illusion of reality seems unlikely to survive at all in the reader's memory of the story. In the fourth chapter there is a fairly detailed account of Allworthy's estate and the surrounding countryside—yet this never proves relevant to anything in the ensuing action. Allworthy himself has earlier been described as a widower and the father of three deceased children—but there is no further reference to his ill-starred family. It is hard to see how this kind of information can become a living part of the narrative when it bears no relation to the story which is being told.

This kind of piecemeal criticism, however, is bound to be fragmentary and subjective, and seems unlikely to lead to any general conclusion. A more comprehensive approach to the problem may be suggested by an analogy from the visual arts concerning the way in which a painter's audience is likely to interpret the information he puts before them. In *Art and Illusion* Professor Gombrich devotes several chapters to a consideration of how a picture is 'read'—how the various patches of paint on a canvas come to be seen as representa-tions of trees or clouds or people. It is shown that the man who looks at a picture has a natural tendency to assist in the illusion that is being presented to him. He will expect to see the colours concerned as a coherent pattern, and will as far as possible relegate to the background elements which are irrelevant to this pattern or which would impair it.

It seems likely that the way in which we react to the novel is a cognate process. We are so conditioned to reading a story in terms of a sustained illusion of reality, that only the most positive efforts on the part of the author could persuade us to view a narrative disjunctively. But there is the one obvious difference between the reading of a narrative and the 'reading' of a painting, that whereas the latter is characteristically an instantaneous process, in which the various constituent elements fuse into a distinct pattern at a glance, the former procedure is necessarily linear—the illusion cannot immediately be sensed, but defines itself as it emerges.

It is impossible to state precisely, even in the case of a single work, what the illusion created by a novel consists in. But the traditional idea that the novelist 'creates a world' suggests a clue. A novelist cannot handle all the eventualities and kinds of behaviour to be found in real life, but he can produce a lifelike effect by working with a limited number, mutually consistent. In theory his readers will not be able to make a certain judgement about the range within which he has decided to work until they have read the whole of the given novel. But in practice the general tendency of the action will suggest from the first the limits the author has set himself, and the way in which he tells his story will reinforce this suggestion. The illusion created by a novel, then, defines itself by an interaction of plot and tone. This interaction provides certain criteria for the automatic sorting process which the reader carries out as he goes through the novel. He is able to 'place' each episode in terms of the emerging pattern.

The fact that the novel produces a consecutive, and not an instantaneous, effect gives the novelist an advantage which the painter does not have. If a painting contains information at odds with the prevailing illusion the observer may register it as a disturbance—may have to make a deliberate effort to disregard it. But the reader of a novel, encountering items of information successively, can have little immediate certainty about the importance of the individual item. Each episode must be filed away in his memory. If it eventually proves to be unnecessary or discordant it may well be forgotten altogether. At first it seems possible that the description of Allworthy's estate and the account of his married life will prove significant to the story to follow. But as chapter follows chapter without either subject being referred to again, the information gradually recedes. Perhaps not one reader in ten will remember by the end of the book that Allworthy is a widower.

At first sight this winnowing process seems to operate only in Fielding's favour. The information he assembles rather haphazardly, without making overall coherence a primary consideration, is conveniently pruned and shaped for him by the subconscious of the modern reader. In fact, however, there is a considerable loss entailed. The reader who is interpreting an episode as a contribution to the illusion created by the novel as a whole is less likely to notice any intrinsic point it may be making. Part of Fielding's didactic intention is therefore liable to remain unfulfilled.

The major drawback, however, is something subtler and more serious than this. Fielding has often been praised for his use of irony and ambiguity—for the way in which he leaves the reader to draw many significant conclusions for himself. Often the author passes no final judgement on a character or situation. Often he suggests several possible points of view, implying that all of them would have to be taken into account in a fair estimate. It has been claimed that much of the richness and complexity of the novels derives from unresolved tensions between conflicting ways of looking at a single character or incident.

It may be argued, parenthetically, that Fielding sometimes makes a self-indulgent use of this sort of ambivalence. He gets a great deal of broad comedy out of Western by portraying him as the familiar booby-squire of artificial comedy, but he interpolates an account of his married life that is ruthlessly realistic. It happens to be convenient to the story that is being told that Western is both a comic character and a brutish sot, but what impression of his personality does

Fielding want the reader to take away? In this case the two possible readings cannot easily be reconciled: Western must be either basically endearing or basically repellant. By posing these alternatives without further explanation Fielding is evading a responsibility.

But the real weakness of this technique only becomes apparent when *Tom Jones* is considered in terms of the way it works as a totality. It has already been suggested that the plot and tone of the book will play the major part in determining what items of information the reader is likely to register as important, and what he is likely to relegate to the back of his mind as subsidiary. What frequently happens, therefore, is that of several possible readings left open by Fielding's irony only one survives in practice since it is the only one endorsed by the working of the text as a whole. To take two examples: there are a number of passages describing the tender nature of Tom's feelings for Molly Seagrim. Yet in general the part she plays is the familiar one of the comic whore. Tom's affair with Mrs. Waters at Upton is narrated lightly enough—in fact it is made the source of a series of farcical scenes. Later in the story, however, Tom comes to believe that he was committing incest. In retrospect the episode takes on a different character, potentially horrifying. Now it can be argued that these are two cases where Fielding points to a moral complexity without trying to resolve it. From one aspect Molly may be a whore, but from another she may be an object of love or compassion. Tom's night with Mrs. Waters may have seemed good fun at the time, but it could have led to tragedy. Tom was being irresponsible.

But the narrative illusion produced by *Tom Jones* as a totality admits in each of these cases only one of the possible readings. The reason is clear—in Professor Gombrich's words: 'Ambiguity cannot be seen.' While subject to the illusion created by a painting, we cannot *simultaneously* be aware that some element in it could be differently interpreted if considered outside the context of the illusion. The plot of *Tom Jones*, incorporating so much that is artificial and far-fetched, and its tone, light and often facetious, suggest that Fielding is claiming for his work only a limited seriousness, a limited reference to real-life standards of probability and morality. Conditioned to this level of response the ordinary reader will tend towards the simplest reading to the exclusion of the others. The night at Upton will seem good fun, and nothing worse: Molly will seem a comic whore, and nothing better. To generalize a point which seems relevant to criticism of the Novel in general: traditional methods of local analysis fail to allow for the fact that the part so analysed will be modified by its relationship to the novel as a whole. And it is basic to the way in which novels are written and to the way in which we respond to them, that the effect of the whole will predominate at the expense of that of the part.

The above comments on *Tom Jones* run counter to a notable trend in Fielding criticism. Professor Crane, for example, would see the limitation in the reader's response as a tribute to the author's controlling skill. If the reader never really believes that Tom will prove guilty of incest, this is because the book is, after all, a comedy. The incident may have serious implications, but these must not disturb the comic surface of the novel. It is precisely Fielding's careful adjustment of manner and matter that gives the book its remarkable unity.

But to accept this argument is to assume a control of narrative effects unlikely in an author experimenting in a brand-new form and preoccupied with the problem of projecting certain didactic views. Fielding would scarcely have been satisfied to evoke a general response too lighthearted to take in even the basic moral of *Tom Jones*—the need for prudence—and still less the continual flow of detailed ethical comment that the novel was designed to accommodate. Yet the moral seriousness of the book was not generally appreciated for a century and a half. The harmony that Crane finds is surely not the harmony that the author planned for his novel as a whole, but the harmony of the illusion that the modern reader finds in the story: something much simpler than Fielding intended.

To answer the question posed at the beginning of this chapter: the effect of the artificial elements in the novel is to persuade the reader that the narrative functions on the level of reality of, say, a Rowlandson print. Hence the difference between the response of the critic and that of the ordinary reader will inevitably be a radical one. The local subtleties which the former can find are often inoperative in an overall reading.

It happens, then, that although Fielding's novels tacitly lay claim to a prevailing moral delicacy and alertness, this complexity of approach is in practice often vitiated by the broad artificial comedy and the complex plotting which are also fundamental to his programme. Consequently it is hardly surprising that his novels do not succeed at quite the level at which they were intended to succeed. But it is surprising that there has been so comparatively little critical awareness of the interesting gap between intention and achievement. This may be taken as a tribute to the degree of success which Fielding does attain, or as a demonstration of the extent to which the novel has come to be automatically interpreted in terms of the illusion it creates.

It would be misleading, as well as ungrateful, to close the argument here. If, as this chapter has implied, Fielding's critics have in a sense overestimated his novels, it is because they have underestimated the extraordinary breadth of his theoretical scheme. His new form was intended at once to instruct and to entertain, and it was to do both by giving full scope to the author's personality as moralist, scholar, humorist, reformer, satirist and man of the world. The novels are epic in their comprehensiveness.

Very few, even of the most eminent English novelists, could have sustained this kind of programme. Fortunately Fielding had a personality rich enough to justify such full-scale exposure, and honourable enough to survive it. But the experiment might nevertheless have proved a failure. The major risk was not that the very various constituent parts would fail to cohere in terms of 'formal realism' or 'narrative illusion', but that they might fail to coalesce into any kind of unified undertaking whatsoever. Fielding might have produced, not a novel, but a box of tricks—a kind of premature, more serious *Tristram Shandy*. But in the event, of course, he achieves this preliminary unity with complete assurance. His main story has a sustained development and animation which draws the reader into, and through, the numerous digressions. The digressions themselves, though diverse in nature and purpose, are linked not only by an underlying consistency of attitude, but also by a consistent tone of voice.

The bustling plot of *Tom Jones*, then, though in one sense inhibiting the realization of Fielding's intentions, does provide a centripetal vigour which holds the book together. The smoothness of tone that reduces the impact of certain episodes does help to blend Fielding's multifarious kinds of comment on life and human nature. The attenuation of the narrative illusion, therefore, seems almost a condition of the novel's succeeding in a simpler and more necessary way.

These unifying tendencies are of particular importance in Fielding's work because he was aiming at extensive effects, requiring a great variety of experiment. By contrast Richardson's powerful intensive effects could be achieved within a relatively restricted form. But Fielding's concern to make his heterogeneous methods of entertainment and instruction relate to a consistently unfolding story is also an advantage in absolute terms. Richardson's dropsical works, for all their remarkable qualities, only spasmodically generate the narrative energy which would be necessary throughout if they were to justify their length. The critic, as in some sense a professional reader, is the very person likely to overlook the critical significance of the fact that Fielding's novels are still read for pleasure.

INDEX